Still Living ... A Great Life

Staying Sane in an Insane World

Reflections over Tea & Custard Creams

Written & Illustrated

By

Denise Fedigan

Copyright 2022

CONTENTS

Preface

Preface

If you are taking precious time to read my book, Thank you!

I am a child emanating from the Maloney and Kenyon tribes, originally from Wallgate and Ince respectively. I have a wide extended family in the Wigan area, and I am a person who keeps in touch. The Kenyon tribe are very close, so if you hurt one, you hurt them all even if you have not had contact for years. I am married to John, affectionately known as Murph or my sweetheart! I may also sometimes refer to him in here as my OH ...

I have a passion for family and like to investigate family connections, usually if I stand in a bus queue, I end up related to half of the people there.

I also have a good memory for faces and names, I was once in Manchester Airport and happened upon a chap whom I recalled as a past contact. My sweetheart looked on bemused as I tried to establish with the man how exactly we knew each other? After going through the rigmarole of who what when and where, he said to me:
"Let me put you out of your misery love, I'm Seth Armstrong off Emmerdale."

It is not intended to be a from beginning to end life story, rather a collection of memories and reflections on various times and themes. Each chapter can be read individually, in whatever order you fancy. If you're wondering why Tea and Custard Creams? Well, it's a bit of a standing joke in the family really, firstly, I drink an inordinate amount of Tetley's, also, it relates to my sweetheart's assertion that my job as a Health Visitor was a nice little job ... all Tea and Custard Creams!

The book came about because of my wish that I had recorded or written down many of the tales and conversations I had with my mum, dad, and other precious folks, before they toddled off this mortal coil! The result is, I now realise I'm eventually going to toddle off too. The global "C" word pandemic of 2020 made me realise even more how fragile life really is. I get great pleasure out of the little things in life. But I'm mainly writing it for the hell of it, to give my version, how I saw it, and in some ways how I see it now.

It is personal and it's written from my heart. Maybe it will help you to understand the person I am. I hope it will make you smile, the following quote from Thomas L. Odem really sums it up nicely.

"I have no desire to move mountains, construct monuments, or leave behind in my wake, material evidence of my being. But in the final recollection, if the essence of my being has caused a smile to appear on your face, or a touch of joy within your heart ... Then in living, I have made my mark."

I hope you will get some pleasure out of it. If you don't know me, let me tell you, yes, I'm a bit eccentric and old fashioned, but I have a great sense of humour!

Before I go, let me invite you to read the words of Leanne Womack in her song.

"I hope you Dance."

That is what I hope for you.

Chapter 1

To Write or Not to Write, that is the question?

In the words of Stephen King
"I write so I know what I think."

It's not unusual for me to write, in fact, I find it very therapeutic and relaxing, scribing everything down, and have done for many moons now. In every job I've ever had, folks have commented on my note writing. Before computers, I was almost always the person who did the lettering on posters and signs.

I keep notebooks which house all sorts of what you might think is irrelevant information, but to me they are memory gold. When one is full, I review it and transfer any stuff I want to keep into my next book, sometimes I just remove the irrelevant pages and keep the half-demolished book...
Poetry has become close to my heart, I really don't know where my love of poetry came from, but sometimes, depending on which way the wind blows, it rolls off my tongue. I also paint/ illustrate my work. If you had asked me at 14 if I could write a book, I'd have laughed!
That's why I'm incredibly proud to have published two books so far:
A collection of my poems entitled:
"In the Blink of an Eye"
An children's illustrated story called:
"The Eaglesfield Visitor"

I've been exploring what it is about writing? When I write, I record lots of things that are going round in my head and putting them down on paper simply files them away. I don't have to keep them in my memory bank anymore. I usually record all the relevant stuff, so for me writing is putting my thoughts into a filing cabinet.

I particularly like Snail Mail, written with a black ink fountain pen. Strange, very strange you might think. There's something very special about a handwritten letter.

I think it started when I was a child. My maternal grandad had a brother Billy Kenyon, who I only met in my childhood, he lived in Nottingham. It was a place that, as a child I thought was a place so far away that I'd never make it there. I imagine lots of people have an eccentric aunt or uncle who they can relate to.

Great Uncle Billy, a Chartered Accountant, which to me was a grand title and, as a child, I was extremely impressed. Grandad had a black and white picture of Billy, he was tall and slim, dressed in a suit, shirt & tie, I used to imagine what it was like working in his "office".

To cut the story a bit shorter, once I knew his address in West Bridgeford, Nottingham, I started to write letters to him. Maybe I imagined that I might one day be his "secretary". His letters looked like they had been written with a spider's leg and took a lot of interpreting, but grandad helped. We wrote to each other well into my adulthood and I can't remember why it stopped. When mum passed away, I found one of Uncle Billy's letters in her papers, it ignited great memories for me. He was not my only "Pen Pal".

At 11 when I started grammar school, and began to learn German, I became PP with a German girl called Birgitte Zinke and conversed with her for a couple of years in German of course. I have always wanted to visit Germany ever since, but it is still an unmet intention which is high up on my bucket list. I can still speak a bit of German, which came in handy when we had native German customers in our bar in Tenerife. I remember the delight on the face of a lady called Barbara Funke who was a neighbour, when having spoken to me in her best broken English, as I replied in German. My German teacher Mrs. Willetts would have been astounded; she would have probably told you my head was full of sawdust when it came to the German language! Even I wouldn't have backed myself ...

Like Paula Porifki in the film An Officer and A Gentleman, I have always loved a guy in uniform, so it will come as no surprise that I had a PP in the Royal Navy. He was a guy from Chorley called Steve Morrey, Leading Stores Accountant on HMS Ark Royal, it was all around the time when Rod Stewart released 'Sailing" which even now evokes memories for me. We used to meet up when he was on leave, I fondly remember the first day we met, we arranged to meet at Wigan bus station. I don't know why, but we hadn't exchanged photos, and I asked him how I would recognise him? It still makes me smile when he said, "You will know it's me without a doubt". I can still see him stepping down from the Chorley bus in full Naval uniform. There was a time, we might have had a romantic relationship, however, it was not to be. Sadly, he died in a motorcycle accident in the 1970s.

I first developed a liking for letter writing when I discovered a book called "The Letters of Henry Root". He used to compose and send letters to famous people and political leaders. Henry would send £1 with his letter for their "expenses", well worth a read.

I am from an era where written letters were the main method of communication before technology took over, and I have never been able to shake off the delight in getting a handwritten letter or postcard. I love the Christmas season, receiving cards, it is sad to say, I usually study the envelope before opening and try to decide whose handwriting it is when it comes to other celebrations, I simply don't think an electronic greeting, thumbs up or smiley face happy birthday is the same when it comes from a close friend or relative.

I'm no dinosaur, but sometimes technological improvements simply aren't improvements.
Facebook greetings are nice to be nice ....
To me they don't carry the same sentiment....

Having dragged myself into the 21st Century, I'm proud to say this Silver Surfer has her own blog:
www.millyismetresfrommadness.com
"Ramblings of a retired nurse staying sane in an insane world."

I sometimes put stuff in emails to record what happened in any given situation, then mail it to myself. I'm very technologically savvy by the way, not just a hat stand!

Some of my favourite Apps are notepad or pages on iPad where I write letters then decide if I want to send them. These are especially letters of complaint, if I want to "sound off" I just write or use voice recorder to type for me.

I don't need to worry about whether my grammar or punctuation is correct, and it makes me smile when I read it back or edit it. So, a note for my nearest & dearest, if you find a letter addressed to you on my iPad, take a deep breath, it might be a complaint!

An example of this is a letter I wrote to the hospital after my mother passed away. As a retired nurse, I suppose I judged the care she received starkly, especially as it was mum. It was not unreasonable criticism; I simply wrote a letter to the staff on the wards where my mum was cared for. It was not easy reading and I still find it very painful to think back about what happened. As I know it's all recorded in the letter, I don't think about it so much. It helped me to deal with my bereavement. If you have something which is troubling you, if you're not really computer savvy, try writing it down anywhere even on a little bit of paper, fold it up and put it in a box and put the lid on. Put the box away, it will surprise you how it clears your mind!

I didn't post the letter of complaint about my mum's care, simply keep my thoughts for posterity. It would have caused me more upset to go through the complaints procedure and listen to the powers that be trying to justify and defend what happened.

One of my favourite pastimes is to send postcards, out of the blue. "Sending a hug in the post" it gives me great pleasure thinking of the response of the recipient, surprised by a handwritten postcard. I have recently been sending old fashioned songs from www.thepostcardshop.co.uk

13

They are just fab. It gives the first line of the song, and I can imagine people seeing it and breaking out in song, especially my older friends.

It reminds me of my childhood when people went on holiday. Of course, there were no mobiles, (OMG ... How ever did we cope, ... Lol) I was well in my teens when we got a house phone, (funnily enough, I still remember Wigan 217251) and above all.... no social media.

We used to be delighted when our relations sent saucy postcards and beautiful views of where they were staying. It would brighten the day when they dropped on the mat.

So, if you ever receive an anonymous postcard, just smile and imagine it's me!

I feel a diversion coming on ....

I've just had another thought when I remember no mobiles, its difficult to imagine in this technological age, if you had a friend who was lucky enough to have a home phone, you could visit the local 'phone box' and call them.

It was 2p to make a call, so you rang the number, you got a beeping sound when they answered, and you pushed your 2p in the slot. Your 2p would give you several minutes, how many, I can't remember, anyway when your money was about to run out, you would hear what was commonly known as the pips ... Beep ... beep ... beep and if you were luck enough to have another 2p to carry on talking you would push it in the slot. There were a lot of conversations cut short,

I'm smiling just thinking about this.

If there was a problem getting through or losing your money, you would phone 'the operator', usually a friendly woman sat somewhere in a telephone exchange who would put you through. If you were very savvy, you could save your 2p for the penny tray in the shop, and tell the operator you had lost your money and get through for free, Lol ... did that more than a few times.

Chapter 2

The Maloney Branch

My paternal Nan & Grandad were Esther and Tom Maloney who were more of a traditional, old-fashioned couple. They were very kindhearted, but strict in their ways and beliefs. Grandad ruled the roost. Both Nan and Grandad were born in 1900.

They originated from Wallgate, Wigan. Grandad worked on British Rail in the engine yards, engineering. Nan was kept busy at home with the kids (14), and she would do a bit of cleaning later in her life.

Nan and grandad lived in a three-bedroom house with a bathroom on a council estate. They and their family were the first, and only tenants to ever live at that address. My Aunty Joyce bought the house under the right to buy from Wigan council and only recently had to move into a nursing home (aged 81) after my uncle Raymond sadly died suddenly in Jan 2021.

Dad was thirteenth of fourteen children, Aunty Joyce being number 14. I remember a conversation with nan as a teenager, about their large family. Mostly responses were clothed in humour:

"Every time he hung his pants up on the bed, I was pregnant."

She had a lot of children keeping her occupied and I should imagine didn't have much time to think about post-natal depression. It would undoubtedly have been an acceptable part of motherhood. As far as I'm aware, she had her first child in 1924 and her youngest child in 1940, so in 16 years, she carried and birthed 14 children, Phew! In all those years, she would have been pregnant for 124 months, or almost ten and a half years!

Of their fourteen children, sadly, Nan had two sets of twins stillborn. It must have been mentally exceedingly difficult for her. If you consider the incidence of post-natal depression, how must women in Nan's time got through? Added to which, she must have struggled with bereavement when she lost children through illness and accidents.

Back in early part of the 20th century, the infant mortality rate was extremely high due to poor maternity care, childhood diseases and other causes. Before July 1948, mothers wishing to have a doctor in attendance at childbirth had to pay not only his fee, but also for any medicine they required.

There was a peak in the births following the end of WW1. In 1920 approx. 950,000 births were recorded.

Sadly between 1901 and 1930 an average of 1:10 babies died. Bronchitis and Pneumonia were the main causes of death in infancy and childhood between 1920-30. The five main diseases accounting for 1:2 deaths were pneumonia, TB, Diphtheria, Measles and Whooping cough. These are diseases mainly wiped out by immunisation, however, the MMR Vaccine received such bad press that those diseases have become prevalent again.

Believe it or not but in the 60s, where a child got measles, it was thought a good idea to have a party to expose other children to the disease. They were known as "measles parties." Measles is not a cute, harmless Kiddies disease by any stretch of the imagination. In 2018, according to the WHO, an estimated 140,000 people worldwide died from measles. Most deaths were in children under five. Measles and mumps can lead to encephalitis or inflammation of the brain. Although the numbers of actual deaths in the UK are minimal, in developing countries mothers don't count on their children surviving until after they have survived measles.

Ten of dad's older siblings died young. Two died in a house fire, when nan had "nipped to a neighbours house". During the fire, my dads' older brother, uncle Jim who was the oldest child in the house at aged 6 or 7 rescued his little sister Margaret who was two and a half. I have a cousin, Margaret, named after her.

After speaking with Margaret, she told me the coroner's report cited Uncle Jim, a very brave little boy. I'm not sure of why so many of nan's children died, I only ever knew three of dad's brothers and sisters. My memories of Uncle Jim were of a quietly spoken, gentle man and his lovely wife, Aunty Flo, about 4ft 10 of sheer delight, I loved her with a passion! One of my abiding memories was a gift of a Spirograph on Christmas, and a canary yellow linen dress which Aunty Flo gifted me, just wonderful!

Dad's sisters, Aunty Joyce and Aunty Winnie, both very down to earth, each had Grandad's gingery streak.

Every little girl remembers the day she became a bridesmaid I think, mine was in a peach satin dress at the wedding of aunty Joyce and Uncle Ray. I remember vividly going to the shop of a dressmaker called Ellen Rowe as a child for measurement and fitting of dresses for the wedding. It was magical, I can still remember the smell of the fabric in the shop. It was one of those days I will remember forever, that and when I made my First holy Communion. It's incredible how my brain remembers and links the memory through the smell of fabric.

Aunty Winnie was a firecracker with a shock of red hair, I only met her when I was 16 as there had been a rift in the family over Winnie's husband Tommy not standing when the priest visited (incredible, but that's how it was back in the day). She was the most friendly, helpful person with an infectious laugh. I was lucky to develop a close relationship with her from my teens until she died a few years ago.

I digress ...

Nan told me that my dad was only 3lbs born, I only recently discovered that he was a twin to a sibling that died at birth. She wrapped dad in a blanket and put him in a box at the side of the fireplace and gave him brandy off a spoon. She thought he was going to pass away. It must have been heartbreaking for her to think her baby would die, especially as he had survived a twin birth. I'm not sure if the brandy was to anaesthetise him and help him on his way. Thankfully, he survived. I always used to joke with him that as he started drinking at such an early age, he had developed bad legs... They wouldn't walk past pubs!

I have often wondered whether nan bonded with my dad after expecting him to die, as there was a time when dad told me that he thought he was seen as the "Black sheep of the family." I don't think he was very close to her. It was true in my experience, and relationship with dad that he was dogged with poor self-esteem and mental health throughout his adult life. I wonder if it harked back to his entry into the world. Something I'll never know ...

In those days, it was a very patriarchal world, and I noticed the male dominated culture and the impact it had on my female relatives. The women generally had to gain their husbands permission to do practically anything apart from working and looking after the family.

One of the other "jobs" women did was to prepare the corpses of people who had died, for funeral. Nan was one of the women who attended to the dead in her neighbourhood. It was customary to wash the body, ensure the eyes were closed and clothe it in a white garment "To meet The Lamb of God." Most corpses lay in the house between death and burial. Rooms would be "dressed" in white sheets and flowers for the "Laying Out". Many of my older female relatives over the years have had cupboards containing linens and such like for use when they died. I was really surprised to hear, when a friend told me that the tradition is still carried on in Liverpool. Funnily enough, when I was a student nurse, one Sunday afternoon there was a knock on the front door. A neighbour had called to ask mum if I could help her to "lay out" an elderly gentleman who had been found dead sat up in bed a few doors down. Dad joked and asked if it counted as a foreigner ... lol

Despite the male domination, back in the early 60s, the women in my family mostly accepted the culture and seemed happy with their lot. It was acceptable that the men folks went to the club, and only returned when they had their fill, often pissed if you'll excuse the term! I remember mum telling me that my dad had refused to allow her to go on a coach trip to Blackpool, with his own mother and sister.

Things changed as I grew up, I was not so accepting and empowered my own mum to forge change.

In the beginning of mum and dad's marriage from when I was born in 1958 until 1965, they both worked full time to "get on their feet". They had moved through several addresses, first living with dad's parents which was customary in those days. It was noticeably short lived, literally a matter of weeks as in mum's words...

"I would have strangled her (nan) if we hadn't moved out."

They took lodgings with a lovely man, a widower, called Harold Leach, who lived across the street at number 23 Almond Grove and was the place I was born. He would have been approaching 74 when I was born. He adopted me as his granddaughter and became my 3rd Grandad. That is a tale in itself....

Eventually we moved to Kitt Green and settled in our family home in 1965. A brand new, just built, council house with all mod cons. Mum and dad lived at that address for the rest of their lives. It was our family home until mum passed away in 2019.

In order that they could work, I would stay with dad's parents Mon-Fri, it was a strict household, Grandad was the "Boss". My grandparents were kind people, I think they always had good intentions. I liked living with them and they would treat me taking me with them on lovely holidays to Great Yarmouth.

I became partner in crime to Esther, my paternal grandmother, affectionately known as "Nanny."

Nanny used to keep chickens in the yard, we had cats too, amazingly living alongside the chooks. She would take me on the train to Manchester where we would shop the markets.

She would buy little yellow chicks, balls of fluff, to rear in the garden. Nan transported them back on the train in her shopping bag, she would let me hold and cuddle one in my pocket. I felt like the bee's knees, little did I know that they would end up in the pan.

As her sidekick, she would tell me what to tell Grandad if there was any bother, to back her up, and keep her out of trouble.

It was the kind of household where grandad knew what he would be eating on a particular day of the week.

He worked on the railway, and tea would have to be literally "on the table" as soon as he arrived. He was a very tall, thick set chap with a ruddy complexion and freckles. His red-grey hair was thinning on top with a comb over.

Grandad had a lovely smile; he was always very kind to me looking back. My evenings were punctuated daily by a boiled egg for supper followed by a tale told from his memory. It was strictly bed at 8pm. Jam butties delivered by hand through the railings at school play time added to my love for him.

When it came to Nan, he had her running round after him like a headless chicken. She would attend to his every whim; he would shout from the table.... "Salt, Pepper, knife, fork, bread, butter" I don't know why, she never seemed to learn and just make sure everything was on hand, as this was a daily exercise. He had a pint pot of black tea, with 3 sugars. Nan would have to make it an hour before he landed because he liked it cold.

I can't remember what day of the week was "Steak" day, and I distinctly remember one day, as we got in after coming home from school, nan walked into the kitchen and went to get grandad's steak off the slab. There were no fridges back then, so fresh stuff was kept on a cold larder slab.

As I followed her into the kitchen, it quickly became apparent that the slab was bare, and she flew across to the window and out into the garden. The cat had the steak, dragging it through to garden, through the rose bushes, across the veg patch. As it caught sight of Nanny, it took off at speed over the fence into the neighbour's garden. In the blink of an eye, she was over the fence. Like a heat seeking missile, she stalked and chased him, her pinnie flapping as she raced round the garden, but sure enough, she cornered him. I bet the cat regretted his adventure as she got him by the scruff of the neck. All the chooks were squawking and flapping as the cat got a good hiding and flew off over the fence.

She turned around, steak in one hand and straightening herself up said to me "Don't tell him!", it still makes me smile. She took the steak inside, rinsed it under the tap and remarked "Bobs your uncle" as she lay it in the pan ready to be served up later. As agreed, her partner in crime kept shtum.

The steak incident reminds me of the scene in Shirley Valentine. Emotionally distant husband, Joe, who liked a certain meal on a certain day was presented with chips and egg on "steak" day. Shirley had fed his steak to her friend's vegetarian bloodhound, very funny! I often witnessed grandad throw the plate "up the coal hole" if it wasn't as expected. Nan would be quaking in her boots at his temper.

Having said that, she was a very strong character, she could hold her own.... but not with grandad.

25

I experienced some adventures particularly with Nan, on trips out. I call them adventures because there would always be some drama involved. We were usually accompanied by my cousin Alan, and Aunty Alice, nan's sister. Alice was a very small-framed, round-shouldered woman in comparison to nan, Alice always wore a headscarf. She had a sweet smell about her, not like perfume, rather like sweet breath as though she was diabetic. She used to grab my cheeks and dive in to kiss me when we met. We would catch the train, we got free passes for travel as grandad worked on the railway. Nan would always pay for our days out, from her big purse in her big handbag.... She never seemed short of money.

Alice wasn't well off. I remember being horrified when I overheard her telling nan that her son had been sent to jail for burgling houses. Even then, I had a sense of social responsibility.

On the train, the ladies would sit nattering away, catching up, and Alan and I would sit side by side looking out of the window watching for Blackpool Tower.

There was no end of excitement, it was like travelling to the other side of the world. We would usually go to Blackpool, because nan had a nephew who lived in Lytham St Anne's, Uncle Edward, whom she had brought up after his mother died. He was a chef at Wharton Air Base, very impressive! I used to think they were posh!

We would often go and visit him and Aunty Jean, followed by an adventure in Blackpool. I loved it in Lytham, it was like a different world, their house was fancy by our standards.

Aunty Jean, a jolly lady always made good butties followed by biscuits and flat top milk to drink, not the usual "Steri."

She always took us on the park while Nan caught up with Uncle Edward, a real treat!

There was a particular trip that really stands out, having done our visiting, nan treated us to donkey rides, slot machines and a ride on the fair.

After fish and chips on the front, this particular day, we walked right up North to "Uncle Toms Cabin".

"This is our time now kids, you sit on the step, Aunty Alice and I are just going to have a gill."

Alan was older, so he was charged with keeping an eye on me. We were well catered for, bottles of pop and bags of crisps in abundance.

As dusk turned into darkness, eventually, nan and Alice fair floated out of the pub full of whisky, and we made our way to the station.

Unsurprisingly, looking back, we had missed the train and, nan considering alternative options, decided we would get the bus to Preston where we maybe would get a train going forward.

I had no idea what time it was but in our usual happy go lucky way, Alan and I went with the flow, taking it all in.

Preston bus station was pitch black and deserted when we arrived, in fact, the bus we were on went straight to the bus wash where we woke up on the back seat.

There were no phones in those days, so ringing anyone was out of the question. There was no possibility of anyone coming to pick us up because no one knew we were there. In any case, I don't think at that time anyone in the family even owned a car!

Without further ado, we went to the Train Station, and discovering the next train was the 4am milk train, nan bedded us down in the waiting room and we travelled home with the flat top!

By the time we reached Almond Grove, grandad was sat in the window, elbows on the table, head in his hands. As he clocked us, he bolted out of the house, hands on hips.

Nan nudged me... "Don't forget what I told you."

Alan and I had been fully briefed that we had stayed at Uncle Edward's and, as he arose early for work, we got the first train out.

Grandad shook his head and bellowed....

"Esther, don't tell me any lies!"

"I'm not going to" she replied and pointed to me...

"Denise, tell grandad where we've been."

Checkmate!

Apart from when facing grandad, nan was not a woman to be messed with, I remember dad getting a phone call in early 1974. When he answered, his face dropped, and it was clear it was not good news. He was listening intently and then said:

"You mean mother has been mugged?"

It was obvious he was shocked. Mum and I stood waiting with bated breath to hear if she was ok.

There appeared visible softening of his worried stare, it soon became apparent that she had been attacked after getting off the bus coming home from Bingo. A youth came out of an alleyway and attempted to steal her bag as she entered the street. Without further ado she had decided he was not going to escape and had grabbed him by the scruff of the neck and clobbered him with her "big handbag". The mugger scarpered, after all she had had experience chasing a cat and the handbag was more precious than the steak. I imagine he kept it quiet, it's not often a mugger is fought off by a 74-year-old.

Nan lived to be 89 years old and had outlived grandad by 17 years. Back in the day, people used to always have life policies to leave to pay for the funeral. The insurance man would knock on the door every Friday to collect the money and make an entry of payment in a little book, which nan kept on the sideboard.

After several years, they became "paid up policies". This meant that whilst no more premiums were paid, they would pay out on death.

So, in December 1989, nan passed a away peacefully at home. My Aunty who lived with nan, called the insurance company to make a claim on her life insurance.

The "insurance man" called round a few days later. He sat on the settee looking apologetic, and announced,

"I don't know how to break the news... your mother cashed in her life insurance when she was 74."

Touché!

Chapter 3

The Kenyon Branch & Grandad Harold

My maternal Grandma & Grandad were Clara and Richard Kenyon, truly, a marriage made in heaven. They were very enabling, Grandad treated Gran like the Queen. It was always said they were like Darby & Joan which was a proverbial phrase meaning ...

"A married couple content to share a quiet life of mutual devotion"

They were both very quietly spoken, I don't think I ever heard a cross word between them, nor a bad word said about anyone by either of them. They had a good "partnership" and were always welcoming.

The family originated from Ince, Wigan. Grandma's maiden name was Blakeley.

Grandma and grandad Kenyon were born in 1916 and 1914 respectively. They met whilst working at the coal mine, grandad worked at the coal face and grandma on the pit brow. Women were forbidden to work underground after 1842 when The Mines Act came into being. Prior to that time, even children worked underground. A miner's wage was £3 8s 8 d and pit brow lasses earned the princely sum of 6-8 shillings a week. They had two daughters and a son, the eldest was mum.

Mum had one Sister, the lovely Aunty Joan and a brother, the delightful Uncle Richard, or Rick as he was affectionately known.

Aunty Joan was, and still is like my second mum, like mum, she met her sweetheart Graham, in the mill in Rochdale. I still have happy, abiding memories of spending time in Rochdale at her house in the Summer holidays, it seemed like a million miles from Wigan, there was a farm at the back of the house on Hilltop Drive and we would have views all over the countryside.

Uncle Rick was my first love, I would have married him Lol ... He and his sweetheart Aunty Catherine took me everywhere with them when I was a child. It makes me realise how lucky and blest I am to have such a loving family

It would be amiss not to mention that from 1936-1942, Grandad was also an accomplished professional boxer. Taking part in 42 fights, he recorded a total of 27 wins and 8 draws. He

fought all over the country at lightweight. His brother was manager and accompanied him to all his bouts.

In 1947, grandad had a stroke of amazing luck, he won £1000 on the football pools. If you adjusted his win to consider inflation, it would be equivalent to around £56,000. His win set he and grandma up in a grocer shop business in Hardybutts Wigan, effectively the shop was in the front room of their house. Mum remembered the pools win; she was treated to a doll to mark the occasion!

We only used to see them at weekends because mum and dad worked in the week, and I was at dad's parents' house. By the time I was born, grandad Kenyon was suffering ill health. In 1959, soon after I came along, he was the first person in the country to have replacement valves in his heart via open heart surgery. A surgeon called Mr. Dark operated on him in Manchester, and essentially saved his life. He always reported that Mr. Dark had told him they would last 20 years, and as he got older, was living on borrowed time.... little did I know.

We always went for Sunday dinner, when we moved to Kitt Green in 1965, they lived just down the road. It was wonderful having them close by. Sundays was incredibly special, the door at grandma's would open, and the beautiful aroma of roast leg of lamb would punctuate the air. The kitchen was a hive of activity, the morning work was baking while the joint was roasting. She would lift it out of the oven, and I would see the stock with the fat glistening on top. Grandma used to tell me it was the "essence."

It tasted divine, thickened with corn flour and coloured with old fashioned gravy browning. I remember one day, having a secret spoonful of the 'essence' while grandma had gone in the front. Only thing was, by the time I had done, there was almost no gravy left, good job she had a sense of humour! My love of carrots and turnip also emanate from Grandma Kenyon's cooking skills. Plenty of butter and pepper made them to die for!

There would be an array of golden baked pies and cakes. Gran's favourite bakes were custard pie and apple for after dinner, yum! I was her sous chef, doing the preparation, learning on the job.

Grandad, dad and sometimes my uncles would all go to the Club across the road, which gave us girls a free afternoon to chat in the kitchen. I get a great feeling of warmth thinking of those times. We would listen to Jimmy Clitheroe; he was a great comic entertainer at the time. The Clitheroe kid was a greatly popular radio sitcom where he played a mischievous kid. We used to howl laughing.

When the lads returned after a few pints, we would feast on Grandmas wonderful Sunday dinner and all have a chin wag, play cards and catch up.

Every time we blinked, they had moved, living in nine different addresses round Wigan.

We used to joke they had a bit of gypsy in them, then without further ado, they bought a caravan in Fleetwood and moved in lock stock and barrel. It was great for us, they lived on a holiday camp. It became our top holiday destination. It was next to the ICI chemical plant, and as kids when we stayed with them for holidays, the noise permeated across to the site. Grandad used to joke; it was the giant who lived there flushing the toilet.

I mean, Fleetwood was on the other side of the world

when your transport was in Del Boy (dad's) yellow Reliant Robin. It was great fun, dad was a real joker, he would be "Acting the Mick" as we were packing the car up, "Doreen, don't forget the sink!" We would be packed to the rafters, mum, dad and three kids plus our belongings. It would take hours, all along the "old roads" and warranted a round of applause when the ICI came into vision.

They were the first people on the site to have electricity in their static caravan. It was in a prime location right next to the shower block. Everyone else had gas mantels for light.

Gran had three caravans on the site, we used to stay in one for our holidays, like the one pictured. It wasn't as posh as Grandmas, we had no electric, no TV and it was well before the birth of Wi-Fi. It would be deadly quiet in there except for the background sound of the battery-operated radio. The lights were gas mantels run off Calor Gas. The mantel was a delicate little metal mesh rounded off which fitted over the point where the gas came out. You had to light it with a match and every night we would end up sticking a match through the mantle while lighting it, and we would be left in the pitch dark. We always had a kettle on the calor gas that whistled when it was boiling.

Have a look at vintage photos www.cassiefairy.com really took me back in time, captured the scene perfectly.

All the extended family used to come and join us. There were some real jokers among them, my uncle would throw bread on the roof quietly at night so no one would see him, but as soon as it came light in the morning, the sea gulls would be dive bombing, landing for bread and running along the roof to take off.

All the women would make a trip into Fleetwood to the butchers where you could get a £2 wrap. It would consist of every meat we would need for the week's meals, breakfast dinner & tea. We rarely ate out in those days, aside from fish n chips. All the girls would cook and we'd all chuck in helping, peeling and baking. We enjoyed the banter sharing meals together.

We would walk for miles down the leafy lane to Rossall school and across the cow fields to the beach. Mum would be cornered by the cattle, she wasn't very tall (4ft 10), she'd be screaming her head off with her hands over her face, and we would run off screeching laughing. We enjoyed the simple pleasures, games of cricket on the beach, paddling and building ginormous sandcastles, all the adults and kids joined in.

At night we would all go in the club on the caravan site, they had talent and beauty competitions, glamorous granny and knobbly knees. There was a bowling alley where everyone plays against each other, loser had to run round the camp "boundary road" the next day with everybody cheering them on. They were amazing times.

I'm delighted to tell you I had a third grandad, my grandad Harold and I have to apologise for the brevity of this chapter. I'd really like to tell you more but a lot of it was in my early childhood and I don't have a good recollection.

Mum and dad lodged with Harold when I was born in 1958, he was not related by blood, but he became my grandad by love. He was born in 1884 and would've been approaching 74 when I was born. Harold fought for his country in World War 1 with the Lancashire Fusiliers and was taken prisoner by the Japanese. I've often heard people ask the question...
"If you could sit on a bench and chat for an hour with someone from the past or present, who would it be?"
My choice would be Harold.

He died when I was 13, and on reflection I hadn't become grown up by then. Now I'm an adult, I am frustrated that I know very little about him, I don't even have a photo, although I have a vivid picture in my head. He was a widower by the time I was born in 1958. He was about 6ft tall, slim with a sallow complexion, he was very grey, balding on top. He always wore trousers, shirt with grandad collar, waistcoat indoors. He would don a collar

& tie when he was going out, even just to the shops at the bottom of the road. I remember his great coat which he wore daily, topped off with a trilby!

The front room had the most ginormous black leaded fireplace or "grate" as it was known, with an oven on the left side. The mantelpiece or Cornish as we called it, was about 5 feet high. It looked like a giant's house to me.

The living room was quite small but was full of dark wood furniture, a tall dresser with a back like a Welsh dresser adorned with two eagles, wings outspread, on each side as if they were going to fly off. A heavy square table with bulbous legs in front of the dresser crammed everything forward in front of the blazing coal fire. The glowing embers would be backed up the chimney ...

Harold sat in an easy chair to the right of the fireplace invariably with a cup of Camp Coffee in hand. There was a strong chicory coffee aroma in the air. We would sit together, chatting, he would tell me tales about the war and being a prisoner in Japan. After sitting for some time there, my legs would be mottled from the fire

Well before decimalisation, grandad saved piles of pennies for me on the Cornish. I would look up and all the copper would be glinting in the light. He would have a big smile on his face and fill my little hands with what looked like a fortune, it probably was then!

As a little girl, I would accompany him to the grocers where he bought his loose butter, and groceries, and to the post office where he would collect his pension. I would be holding his hand as we strolled along. Looking up, he looked 10 feet tall. On our many trips, we would stop and admire a glass cabinet full of dolls in the post office at "Robin", whilst queueing for the counter. I had my eye on a walking doll, she was almost as big as me and had the most gorgeous blue-lilac floral dress.

I named her Violet; I can see her in my mind's eye. You can imagine my delight when grandad beckoned the assistant to get her out of the cabinet and before I knew it, she was standing beside me.

The excitement was mind blowing as I realised, she was coming home eek! I was about 3 years old. I can still remember smell of the fabric of her dress. It had short, puffed sleeves and she had frilly pants and black shoes. The memory is imprinted on me 55+ years later.

I absolutely loved her, she had a mechanism inside which moved her legs like she was walking, it was magic! It's even bringing me joy remembering.

Sadly, "Violet" became victim of a tragic accident and her porcelain face got broken. I was heartbroken!

Without another thought, grandad put on his overcoat and hat and walked to the post office .... to buy her twin!

It makes me sad to see the property, the former post office, ramshackle and boarded up when I drive by. I still have a vision in my head of a bustling place, everyone queueing for their pensions, chatter filled the air.

When we moved to Kitt Green in 1965, dad worked at Heinz. There was a bus that stopped at the bottom of Almond Grove, number 21, and dropped off just by our new house. For weeks on end, mum would invite

Grandad for Sunday dinner. He was reluctant to get on the bus because he wasn't sure where to get off.

"We'll meet you at the bus stop, go on be a devil!"

It took him till 1968 to make the trip, and after meeting him, he was duly installed in the armchair in front of our new colour telly, which mum and dad rented from Radio Rentals. There was a slot on the back of the telly which took shilling coins. You got so much time per shilling in the slot. The man would come and empty the coin slot on a Friday and collect the rental money. Mum used to look forward to him coming because if there was extra in, above and beyond the rental charge, she'd get it refunded.

I can't remember the reason, maybe he missed the last bus home, but Grandad ended up staying over ... for 18 months! Mum moved my little sister in with me and grandad into her room.

He didn't have a TV at home and settled himself into our routine, it was like a long weekend break which lasted a year and a half! Bless him, he used to stay up till the dot went off the telly (it finished at midnight in those days) then the "Test Card" would be on the screen till it resumed the next day. (The picture on the left is the BBC Test card.) He would remark every night... "It's all a load of twaddle!", he watched when the first moon

landing was broadcast in the summer of 1969 and swore black was white that it was a lie!

He used to ask mum and dad where they were going and what time they would be back Mum used to say...

"He thinks we're his kids" ...

Mum would be hoovering in the living room and Harold would lift one leg, then the other so she could hoover round him lol.

He eventually returned home and settled back into Almond Grove but sadly, he died in 1971 aged 87. I only recently found out where his grave is. I've put on my To Do list to go and find it!

I have one of his war medals and consider it a treasured possession.

I think we were lucky to have him in our lives, he contributed a lot of happiness and great memories, so thanks Harold, you really made a difference, especially to me! ♥

Chapter 4

What do you get when you cross a Maloney with a Kenyon?

A Fedigan ... that's me!

I have some very vivid memories of my early years, I was lucky to have a great relationship with mum and dad and strong bonds with my grandparents, aunts, uncles and cousins on both sides.

My dad was John Benjamin Maloney 8th August 1935 – 20th November 2014, and mum Doreen Clare Kenyon, 15th December 1936 - 21st November 2019.

Our family home was in Marsh Green, Wigan from 1965 until mum died in 2019.

It was a large council estate which occupied a space of approximately a half mile radius. It had a main road running through the middle of it and fields beyond. Marsh Green was hardly a sleepy little backwater, it was like the Wild West at one end of the estate and thankfully a little more salubrious at our end. There would be packs of stray dogs roaming round, kids from toddlers to teenagers on every corner. It was a neighbourly place to live though, most of the families who lived there were at the bottom of the food chain and everyone 'mucked in' If you needed a leg up, everyone would pull together. Mum had a few women friends who also had children and she and they would lend each other money/ ciggies / 2 bob for the electric etc ... basically, if your mam had no bread, then someone else would provide it.

Mum & Dad met whilst working in the cotton mill in Rochdale. Apparently, that's where all the hip people worked back then in the 50s. All the young men & women would jump on the coach at the end of the road at 5am and be transported in. Mum often talked about the "Era", apparently, it was a hotbed of romance! My Aunty Joan and uncle Graham met there too, which lead to her moving and living in Rochdale after getting married. Following the Cotton Mill, dad was a Collier, working at the coal face at Abram Colliery in Plank Lane Leigh. When he came up from the mine, he got himself a "nice little job" working what was then termed continental shifts, at Heinz. His job was keeping the bean gunsons/ tanks filled so that the bean line would keep running. He would have us mesmerised, telling us about the "Magic Eye" which spotted any bad beans, it was unbelievable but true! We nicknamed him Benny the Bean. He spent 22 years at Heinz.

The continental shifts for dad were tortuous, he absolutely hated night shift and we hated it even more. Mum used to call it "silent meals" and she was right. They practically wouldn't speak the whole week.

His difficulty sleeping was the bain of our lives, the least little noise and he would be awake, like a bear with a sore head. As soon as we heard his feet on the bedroom floor, we would scatter. Everything was an effort, nothing was right, mum and I would take time bathing the kids and getting them to bed then mum and I would watch the clock till 9.45pm... dad would silently get his coat on and whoop, party time! Mum would breathe a big sigh of relief and wave as he went through the door.

Funnily enough I had a brief conversation with an elderly lady in the market in the week, she was telling me how fed up she was during the pandemic of people walking round with
"A face like a farmers arse"
It reminded me of mum, she used to say that about dad. Lol!
He would joke about it as night shift week was looming, then boom silence... for a week.

The factory was literally across a field opposite our house so dad could see the house from where he worked. Mum had everything down to a fine art, he would

45

comment what time we went to bed because he could see the lights go out, till we adopted the 'Air raid' rules. Mum used to say,

"When we used to have air raids, we couldn't have lights on because the bombers could see where the houses were" I would listen in awe...

"Well under my rules, Benny can't see the target, so let's see."

We used to stay up just to defy the early to bed rule, Lol.

The air-raid rules really came into their own when I started courting. With dad on nights, the first question would be.

"What time did The Midnight Cowboy go home?"

"About ten" I would say, hoping he hadn't seen the lights of the taxi outside at 1am.

On the other two shifts, mum used to tell me that he would be Happy as Larry, whoever Larry was?

It just occurred to me to Ask Alexa, isn't technology wonderful!

He was Larry Foley, an undefeated Australian middleweight boxer in the 1890s who won large fight garnering prize money of $150,000 dollars. A New Zealand paper went with headline.

'Happy as Larry'

We were, quite understandably brought up on beans, soups and other Heinz delights. Steamed chocolate sponge puddings were a great favourite. There pings into mind, the link with my lifelong love of chocolate. I also remember the introduction to baby's chocolate pudding in tiny tins when my sister Michelle progressed from

Carnation milk to solids. I can picture it now ... a spoon for you, one for me, lol...

I still can't believe that babies were fed on dilute Carnation Milk, mind you it did build her up! and no wonder, full of sugar. The legacy of being brought up on Carnation is that she puts a stone on if she looks at a cream cake lol ...

Dad would bring a big sack full of tins, small and large without labels. Each tin had a code on its lid, so in order to find out what you were opening, you would have to look up the code or simply take a lucky dip. As a kid, I committed to memory every code, and it would be my job to sort them and write on with marker pen so mum would know what was in the cupboards. I still remember most of them 50 odd years later!

Mum moved from cotton mill to a job as a clippie on the cherry and white Wigan Corporation buses. She used to run up and down the stairs on the bus rolling out tickets as passengers got on. In the mornings, I would get on the bus to school, everyone knew mum. I used to think I was really special because I'd get a free ride.

When mum and I went into town, shopping, she would take me into the bus office. It was in the marketplace; we would be sat in the canteen like in the sitcom On the Buses. I used to call the inspector "Blakey" like on the telly. Everybody would laugh and make a fuss of me; we would get a "can of tea" and 2 enameled tin cups like they used to take with them on the bus. Small things still in my memory bank. We would see Bert Bussell, mum's driver, he was a jolly, chunky chap who used to tell everyone that he put mum under his arm and carried her across the road because she was so little. At 4ft 10, she was a little diamond, you know what they say about small things. He would joke that she would fit in his top pocket. The bus inspectors would get on buses randomly and check that people had tickets. The inspector used to ride around changing buses, and you could sense the dread on passengers faces if they had avoided paying. People would run upstairs hoping the conductress or "clippie" hadn't seen them get on. You can see her in the picture at the back of what she used to call a "back loader". It didn't have doors on, just a platform with a rail. I used to laugh when folks ran behind the bus after it had left the stop, trying to jump on. Looking back, it was treacherous! She gave up when she was pregnant early 1966.

She always had loads of tales about the antics of passengers getting on the last bus drunk and refusing to get off. On one such occasion, Bert told her that he would drive straight into the depot with the awkward customers on board. He had tasked her with opening all the upper deck windows where a lot of drunken men had occupied most of the seats and were "Taking the Mick" messing her about when she was trying to get the fares. Bert proceeded to drive through the bus wash. She was howling laughing, describing how all the "drowned rats" soon left when they thought they were on a sinking ship!

After all us kids were on the scene, she always had some part time job or another to contribute to the coffers. Cleaner, barmaid to name but two, working round dad's shifts at Heinz. I was her co-pilot / mother's maid / nursery assistant, Jill of all trades.

Dad gave mum a set amount of money per week from his wages for the House Keeping and she had to manage all the bills, food shopping, utilities etc. In addition, she got 7 shillings a week Family Allowance each Tuesday which she collected with her book from the post office. Her small wage from her part time jobs would supplement the family pot. She would have to feed the gas and electricity meters to keep the lights and other facilities working. The Electric meter took 10p or two bob coins and you would get a certain amount of juice for that, I suppose much like a card meter today.

Sometimes, we would be in the middle of watching something on the telly and click, everywhere would be in darkness, mum would be scrambling about looking for a two-bob piece and dad would be huffin and puffin as he missed the next part of the programme he was watching. There was no catch up, ITV Hub BBC I Player. You were lucky if you had one of those new-fangled video recorders to tape your favourites!

The other complication was that there was also a coin slot on the back of the TV, so if it wasn't the leccy clicking off, the Telly would run out of money!

The silver lining to feeding the meters would be the absolute delight when the man came to empty them. He would pour out all the 10p pieces onto the kitchen table and count them into piles. Mum stood over him like a hawk because, once he had worked out how much was in the meter, he would tell mum how much the bill was, and he would refund her all the cash over and above the bill total. She used to be on cloud nine when she got a rebate. She would say to me, "Don't tell your dad the meter man has been, so she could keep all the rebate", well after all, she was the person who fed the beast! (I mean the meter) Lol.

Dad was extremely strict when it came to boyfriends and going out. Between 16-21, working full time earning a decent wage contributing to the household and had to be in on the last bus. He used to say there's nothing, *interesting to you*, going on after 11 o'clock.

The-world famous Wigan Casino was the hip place to be at the time. In my household, it was out of the question. Well you might be thinking, at 16, I wasn't old enough to drink alcohol, but the truth is, the casino didn't serve alcohol. Soft drinks only, I mean as a parent I can understand his concerns looking back. At the time, it caused me endless frustration, all my friends were hanging out in the trendiest place, and I couldn't go ugh! I was lucky only on a couple of occasions, mum gave me the nod as a treat, when dad was on the graveyard shift People came from miles around on a Saturday night for the northern soul all-nighters. The Casino Club, or the Empress Ballroom as it was formerly known, was it the town centre and was built around the time of the First World War.

The excitement in the queue was palpable, bodies everywhere, boys dressed in Oxford Bags, the anticipation of what was to come. The doors would swing open, and you would look up the steps, 10 deep on every step, all waiting to pay their 75p, get their hand stamped before spilling out into the main ballroom. The massive maple sprung dance floor stretched as far as the eye could see, and beyond it, the stage.

A grand balcony circled the dance floor on three sides, giving a perfect view of the dancers below, dimly lit by ultraviolet tubes hung from the ceiling on chains. It had about a 2000 capacity. Inside it was hardly plush, threadbare carpets, simple old wooden furniture, and disgusting toilets, what it lacked in furnishings, it made up for in atmosphere.

Hundreds of young people from all over the country, dancing, swirling around to Northern Soul music, dance floor springing up and down to the beat, simply magic! You could observe from the balcony, it was electric. The heat, the music, the smell, the condensation dripping from the roof... nothing could, and never will compare to the atmosphere of Wigan Casino. I still get the goosebumps when I hear Dobie Gray, 'Out on the floor' or 'Long after Tonight is All Over'. Have a listen on YouTube!

My other haunt was the Nevada in Bolton on Friday nights. I wasn't allowed to go there either, Lol. I'd make up some story or other and 'escape'. It would be dead exciting; we would get the bus from town to get there for half seven when it opened. It was a military operation, as I strictly had to be on the last bus home. It was two hours twenty-five minutes of bliss, roller skating, smooching, holding hands, under the massive glitter ball

that was the Nevada. I became an accomplished skater, everyone would try to copy the professionals, backwards, forwards, spinning round...

The music would be blasting out, we'd be singing at the top of their voices, well, when we weren't snogging! I would squeeze the last few minutes to the last second, then leg it across to Bolton bus station for the latest bus ... to connect with the last one at 11 to get me home. Breathless, panting, I'd get on just as the doors were about to close, Phew! I still remember mum finding the bus tickets in my pocket, thankfully she didn't tell dad!

I sailed close to the wind sometimes, I don't know if I told you, I have a bit of a soft spot for a guy in uniform, well I got in hot water one night after having a date with a lad who was in the TA. His name was "Nobby" ... Lance Corporal. We had only been 2 miles from home, had a few drinks, but got a bit carried away (with the time) Consequently I missed the bus, OMG, I thought, dad would kill me for sure.

The little action man at my side was not going to be done. He reassured me that, he would take me home to the door, explain to dad and everything would be fine. With an air of confidence, I strode home, soldier by my side, and ended up not that late, except, I was on foot, not on the bus!

As we walked up the road, a figure came into sight, walking towards us. Having my camouflaged friend beside me, was quietly reassuring, I was drowning in adrenaline as I saw dad approaching. I called to him to test the water...

"Hi dad, sorry, I missed the bus."

"Well obviously, ... get in the house!"

Nobby interjected ... "Mr. Maloney.......

Before he had his next word out, dad signalled with his hand and said "About turn soldier" ... I never saw him again...

There was no social media back then, we were lucky to have a phone in the house. If you wanted to speak to someone, often the number you were given to call was a neighbour who was lucky enough to have a phone, and they would go to get the person from next door! The public call box was at the top of the road and if you were lucky, you got through and didn't lose your money lol ... Neither was there social media or internet, we simply had face to face or nothing. If you wanted to see a friend, you would have to walk round to their house and knock on the door.

It wasn't half bad though, we got out of the house and hung out with our mates, we built "dens" where we could meet and when it was coming up to Bonfire night, we would go round collecting wood for the "Bommie" It's just come to mind, we would have to guard our stash of wood because neighbouring kids would watch for an opportunity to "raid" the bonfire wood when you were not on your toes! It would be a competition who had the biggest bonfire.

I eventually did 'settle down' with another uniform and ended up married at 21 in 1979. We married in November 1979 and separated in September 1984. I'll cover it later in the book.

Chapter 5

Bonds Outlasting the Test of Time

I've spent quite a lot of time reflecting on the relationships that I have had and, the memories I still have in my heart today, of my grandparents. It is apparent recalling memories, that my two sets of grandparents were polar opposite in their characters and lives. They each saw situations with different eyes. Nevertheless, they all enriched my life in their own ways and I'm blest to have had such role models / mentors.

Although I am in the autumn of my own life (bit of poetic license there) ... lol, I'm at the "adventure before dementia" stage. I frequently think about them, smile and sometimes shed a tear in memory. Not a bad thing, they still bring joy, even now. I find myself doing things they used to do, like calling someone by the wrong name, or not being able to remember the name of someone I know well.

Back in the 70s when I was growing up as a teenager, it was tradition to see all the "Golden Oldies" as part of the normal week, it was routine.

Grandma Kenyon was an incredible woman she was kind and thoughtful she always had time for everyone. She was a short curvy lady, with bottle blonde hair (bit like me now) Her smile lit up the room, her aura wonderful. She exuded positivity. On reflection she was an emancipated woman in her time, enabled in her relationship by my grandad. She took great pride in her appearance, a real lady. She had a regular hair appointment on a Saturday, and it makes me smile remembering that she had her own personal brush and comb which she took with her. She was particular about not getting nits...Lol.

Obviously when I was a child, she seemed old, when you're 18, everyone is old. The truth is she died at aged 58, 5 years younger than I am now. It still breaks my heart that I lost her at 18, she had a massive heart attack and dropped dead out of the blue.

I remember vividly, it was a Sunday evening in summer, mum was working as a barmaid and dad was on afternoons. There was a knock on the door and my cousin was stood there. It hit me like a ton of bricks when she told me the news, my world stopped turning. She was the first significant person to die in my life. As I looked out of the window a bus passed our house, how could that be? ... grandma had died.

I had seen her the previous day visiting us, but I'd had to rush out. I still regret the times I took for granted she would always be there. I inherited her eternity ring, which I had it remade by a goldsmith, it bears an engraving inside the band ... 'Clara a very special lady', and she truly was.

Individually they all provided a different perspective, observing how they related to each other, the way they spoke. There was always someone to go to for advice, and a wealth of wisdom and experience. They also passed on and kept up family traditions. Grandparents are the family historians; they can relate tales of the past and paint a picture of our ancestors.

Apart from their grocery business in Hardybutts, later in his life grandad had a sweets & tobacco shop in Wallgate, at the end of Miry Lane. In my teens, before I started work, I used to go and help him in the shop on a Saturday. I felt I was the bee's knees, serving behind the counter, filling up the counter and weighing out sweets from massive jars. I would make up his 10p mix bags. He would always give me what he called a little 'back hander' for my hard work.

I remember tales grandad Kenyon told me about his brother David who was his boxing manager. They shared a bed, as back in those days, they lived in a 2 up/2 down, no spare bedrooms, all the kids in 1 room. Topping and tailing was normal. He would say to me that it would be a miracle if he wasn't in the 'deep end', by which he meant he'd avoided sleeping next to one of his siblings who wet the bed. The bedding would be a mixture of woolen blankets topped with an Army greatcoat left over from WW1. It was first in, best spot at the "pillow end" and you never knew who you would wake up next to.

I remember an old friend talking about having overcoats on the bed, he really made me laugh with his jokes ...

"Sleeves in the eiderdown"

57

"I slept with a Japanese General when I was a kid" referring to the Army greatcoat used as a quilt on his bed.

I had a remarkably close friendship with Grandad Kenyon throughout my life, but especially after grandma passed away. He was not in good health with heart and breathing problems. He came to live in a flat close to us so we could be near him. I spent hours on end chatting about his life when I visited. I used to nip down on my bike every night to help him settle, make him a brew, sandwich and leave a flask for later. Turning his bed back, positioning his pillows and ensuring everything was to hand before I left.

On a Saturday afternoon, we would watch the boxing on World of Sport. We would laugh a lot, grandad used to be shadow boxing and talking me through the fight. On one such afternoon, he handed me an envelope containing £200, I was puzzled and emotional. He could see my emotion, he frequently used to say to me after grandma died, that he wished a God would take him. I would joke with him and say,
"He's probably up there disgusted with you saying that."
On that Saturday, he said to me,
"I want you to have that money, I won't be here when you get married."

Sadly, he wasn't, he passed in December 1978 aged 63.
Ironically, he died on the ward where I would eventually become ward Sister at Billinge. The week before he died, I had gone away on my first holiday abroad, to Fuengirola. Little did I know that he would be taken into hospital whilst I was away.

I remember the day we were flying home; I had a "gut feeling" that something wasn't right, simple intuition, I guess. Obviously, there were no mobiles at the time, and I can't remember the circumstances whether I had phoned home while I was away. Mum told me as I landed home at teatime, that Gran was in hospital. She was going to visit, I sent my love with the intention to visit the next day. My gut feeling reminded me that you only regret what you didn't do after she left for the hospital. I was on way 10 minutes later to make visiting time that night. I'm so glad I took the opportunity to see him, it would have been one of my life's biggest regrets to this day. Grandad had passed away by the time we got up in the morning. He certainly was one of the most important people I ever had the pleasure to have in my life.

My grandparents taught me kindness and patience and how routine can keep you on track. Both my grandmothers had great spiritual faith which, although I didn't know it at the time, it would a part of me, later in my life. In coming chapters, you will read about how I was encouraged going into my nursing career and helped by the Bank of Grandad. He taught me that paying back what you borrow can pay dividends!

My number 3 grandad, Harold, stood out as someone who could adopt and love a child as his own grandchild even though we were not blood related. I heard first-hand accounts of experiences of his being a prisoner of war with the Japanese. He was a real gentleman, very quietly spoken and a good listener. I could absolutely kick myself that I don't have a photograph of him, I remember extraordinarily little about his origins, but intend to spend some time exploring soon.

Nan taught me resourcefulness and skills for life. Alongside her mother and homemaker role, she waited hand and foot on grandad, laying out dead bodies, keeping the chickens fed and watered, gardening, she made a few bob, selling home knitted cardigans and pullovers, crocheted covers, paper carnations. I can still knock up a cardigan on the needles and crochet like a good un! She was a strong character, but in her relationship with grandad, she seemed subservient and disempowered. I loved her resilience; we spent many happy hours together just 'living' Her life was a virtual marathon!

In terms of character, Grandad Maloney was a man's man. He wore the trousers, and we all knew it. It wasn't anything out of the ordinary at the time. He wasn't overtly abusive, but he was The Boss. My abiding memory of him was kindness towards me, he had time for me, we chatted a lot across the table as he shared his sugary black tea with me. He would take a shopping bag into town and pick up groceries after he retired which at some point would have been unheard of. I think he mellowed in later life. I remember it wasn't such a song and dance if Nan went to play bingo.

There was something very resilient about their generation, not a lot phased them. I imagine it was because they had endured many challenging times throughout their lives, two world wars, rationing, economic depression, hard work in coal, cotton and heavy manual work on the railway. Added to which, they raised their own children, and often neighbours' children too. It was their responsibility to ensure the elders in the family were cared for. No mean feat, I'd say.

Sadly, although they seemed old when we were young, my grandma & grandad Kenyon were both younger than I am now when they died, 58 and 63 respectively. Nan and grandad Maloney 89 and 72 when they passed away. I've recently learned that Grandad Harold died in 1971 at the age of 87. They were very important influential people, who added a lot of value to my life.

I still hold them all dear to my ♥

Chapter 6

Setting Boundaries and Belonging ...

Don't get Carried Away!

I talk a lot about family, especially mum, and how relationships impact on life for me. To me, family is a group of people related in some way, not necessarily biologically. When I say, 'Belong but don't get Carried Away', what I mean is remember that you also must have boundaries in all your relationships whether family or friends.

All relationships should reach both ways, ideally be balanced, give and take, but sometimes one person takes on most of the responsibility for keeping it going or propping up and doing all the supporting. Don't get me wrong, some people, probably like me, volunteer for everything! In that way, we take it upon ourselves and it's only when you're sliding down the wall with burn-out do you realise … 'actually I don't need to do this'. It's taken me 60+ years to realise Lol. I certainly don't do stuff for reward and I'm not only on about physical tasks, sometimes you can support someone emotionally, giving a listening ear for example. It is more helpful to help the person sort things out for themselves that to do it for them. That way you give them confidence and increased self-esteem. If you always do everything for everyone, then next time they need help, they will come to you. It's called 'making a rod for your own back' in Wigan.

If you imagine that you have so many Yeses and so many Noes in your Good deed bank when you're born, a bit like eggs lol … and you keep them in your heart. When someone wants you to do something for them, you look inside your heart and decide if you have a spare yes or bit of energy to give. You collect yeses and energy when people reciprocate your helpfulness/kindness. So, you can collect from one person and give it to another! That's how support goes round! You collect energy and yeses in all sorts of ways, another example is when you do a good deed, it makes you all fuzzy inside … lol. That's good energy entering your heart …

Never allow yourself to be 'put on' as my mum would say, that doesn't mean being aggressive or fighting, it means being assertive, letting folks know that you have boundaries in a firm but fair way.

Boundaries also help to keep you safe, for example, not allowing people to invade your personal space. This has become very poignant during the Covid pandemic of course, however, it doesn't just apply to physical boundaries, it applies to being respectful and determines how a person treats you and others. Personally, it's a case of your own code of conduct. You have a set of rules which you abide by. Think about what code of conduct you have, it might be influenced, in some ways by the job you do?

When you look back in time, traditionally, families were exceptionally large, my dad was one of 14 children, one of my mum's ancestors had 22 children! (OMG, she would have been pregnant for 16 ½ years) and the family didn't end there. Can you imagine how many pies you would need if the kids came round Lol ... They had massive extended families who all supported each other in different ways. They would all feed each other's kids, even neighbour's kids, all muckin in to bring them up.

I remember my mum talking about her friend Betty Hennesey, she lived a few doors away and was part of a big family. In those days, all the kids would top and tail in bed, so you occupied whatever space you could catch. So, on many occasions, mum and her sister Joan, would go to bed and when they woke in the morning, Betty would be in bed with them.

I was astounded when she told me, but mum thought it was normal, because Betty had gone to get in bed at home and all the kids had spread out, so she went a few doors down where she knew there would be room with mum and Joan ... how crazy!

These days, the politically correct gang would have a field day! My feeling is that family includes any group/place where you feel you belong. A sense of belonging is especially important, part of anyone's life, whether belonging to part of a family/ work group/ church group, craft group, tribe etc ... To belong gives a sense of reassurance, confidence, self-esteem and the feeling that someone has your back.

Whilst you may be biologically related to some people, and love them unconditionally, but not like their behaviour or choices, and to me that is totally acceptable. Even if you love someone, it's about acceptance, not feeling like you must be in control of everything others do. The difference with family is that, in my experience, usually we give more latitude because 'they're family.'

Abraham Maslow, a psychologist penned 'The Theory of Human Motivation' in 1943, he illustrated his theory in the Pyramid or 'Hierarchy of needs', in essence, he identified that there are 5 levels of need. He identified everything starting with human needs like having somewhere safe to live, shelter, food, sleep, clothing etc. Safety and security, respect, self-esteem, if you have all the needs met then you reach self-actualisation/ full potential which in Wiganese is "gerrin there". Love and belonging is one of the important parts which contribute

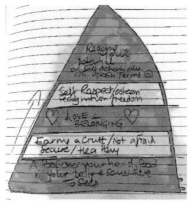

to reaching your potential in life. So, there's a bit of theory behind it, you can find more info on 'tinternet if you've a mind to.

In my case, although it's usually a bit of a joke in my family, the fact I was a nurse, I still belong to that very esteemed group! Even though I am now a vintage nurse, I'm still a member of the tribe! There is a certain affinity between people who hare common interests, it helps self-esteem and confidence.

Anyone who knows anything about Rugby will recognise what I say when I mention the Wigan Tribe and the St. Helen's Tribe, now that really is tribal, even close friends can't talk when one team licks another.

My friend Fiona is a Saints supporter, and it's reasonable to say each team has had its fair share of victories over the other, (Well more Wigan tbh lol). Well, I'm a very arty/crafty person, I've been

Her friends in the knitting box have tied her up, the angel is saying a prayer 🙏🙏 20:05

Get her out and let her watch the match or she will knot all her friends in the box into a roby monster 20:12

You need let her watch the match or she will be sick and

Is she singing and dancing at the moment she is the lucky mascot 👏👏👏

knitting little people and knitted a representation of her in her saint's colours. So little Fiona was in the knitting basket when Wigan played Saints over the weekend! Fiona started what's app messaging me asking if the doll was watching her team win?

It went something like this ...

well you didn't expect me to concede when Wigan were losing ... did you? That's tribalism for you!

67

You only need to have watched the Euros , even those who hate football were cheering, even me .... Football's coming Home ... lol. Slight edit, ya see Football didn't come home in the end, but it lifted the spirits of the country when our boys played out of their skins in the final, sadly to be beaten on penalties. You should take note that people who support a winning team live longer!

So, if you're going to be anything ... be kind! (To yourself too ... but remember to balance it out and accept kindness and help when you need it, it charges your heart up! If you don't charge up, your battery will burn out.

Always remember ... it's ok to say No!

Chapter 7

Started Climbing the Ladder in my Platforms

Work for me, as for many of us, has occupied many waking hours for my entire adult life (and some of my teenage years too. I had many jobs while I was a school including paper rounds and working with the local milk woman from 4am at weekends! I'm fortunate that work has mostly been very enjoyable and has been a big part of my social and personal identity. Starting work was a major turning point in my life and was the start of my love affair with shoes.

Even now, I do all kinds of work to be useful, purposeful, happy and fulfilled. Work for me these days is part time, sometimes voluntary, hobbyist, writer, poet, painter, seamstress, teacher / facilitator... the list is endless. It's not just about money, although back in 1974, my purpose was to buy a pair of platforms...

Looking back, I can recognise the key people who influenced my life from a work perspective, and I recognise that I've contributed a lot to the lives of others. I think that is one of the things we should all realise, every one of us influences others. We don't always realise just how much we contribute. I'm very fond of the 1940s film, "It's a wonderful life" where James Stewart stars as George Bailey. George, is a man who has given up his personal dreams, in order to help others in his community. His thoughts of suicide on Christmas Eve brings about the intervention of his guardian angel Clarence. He shows George how he has touched the lives of others and how different life would be for his wife Mary and his community of Bedford Falls if he had not been born. I know I'm a sentimental old fool! Anyway back to my thread ... lol

In all my jobs I gained valuable and transferable skills that I have used throughout my life. I've been able to explore many avenues but the overriding importance for me is the sense of achievement and purpose.

One of my earliest excursions into the world of work was securing a job as a Saturday girl in the co-op café, it also started my lifetime love affair with shoes! I still remember the smell of the café, and the supervisor Evelyn who took me under her wing. I got my "wages" in a little brown envelope/ pay packet with a see through 'window' in the front, I could see the pound notes. It was a delightful feeling at fourteen, the anticipation that, I could now buy those black and green patent platform shoes!

I spent the greater part of my grammar school education frittering away my time and learning opportunities, in favour of earning a few quid in the kitchen of the Whitesmith pub restaurant opposite my school. It seemed like a good idea at the time, and quite honestly looking back I have a good idea why. I would skip school and would be working at lunchtime when some of my teachers would come in. The boss Eva thought I was such a good little worker volunteering to wash up over dinner, little did she know it was to avoid teachers enjoying lunch in the pub. Don't get me wrong, with hindsight, I recognise that I didn't make the most of my opportunities in education, but I did learn a great deal, nevertheless.

I managed to get myself ejected from the math's class by Sister Margaret Paul who for some reason took a dislike to my platforms. You can't credit it, that I even had the audacity, at 15 to turn up at a Convent school sporting black & green patent shoes. I was a ridiculously small challenge for Sr MP.

I am the eldest of three, being eight years older than my sister and thirteen years between myself and my brother.

When my "little" sister Michelle came along in World Cup winning 1966, just 1 month before the cup final, mum had been in hospital for many weeks because of pregnancy complications. So, the bundle of joy entered the world by Caesarean section 6 weeks premature. She was 4lb 12oz, so at eight I had my own little "doll".

The pregnancy had taken a lot out of mum, so when the baby came home, I was mums "right hand woman".

I still can't get my head round the fact Michelle, a premature baby weighing 4lbs 12oz was fed on Carnation Milk diluted with boiled water. I used to love making up the feeds and would make an extra couple of ounces for myself.

I was a dab hand at feeding, dressing, bathing and putting her to bed. It was a bit of a trial getting this babe off to sleep and she quickly became accustomed to the cot being rocked. Establishing this habit came back to bite me on the ass, as each time I stopped rocking, she would be spark awake which became a bit of a chore when she was a toddler and I wanted to go play put with my mates. I would dread the moment when those eyes opened and the whole routine would have to be gone through again ... I'm still rocking her now. I'm her other 'mother' Ha!

I was quite an established mother's maid by the time my brother Darren made his appearance in 1970. I then had a five-year-old sister and a baby brother; mum would see to the baby, and I'd pacify my sis. Mum had given up her job as a clippie on the buses in 1966, but it was still a big job bringing up three kids on one wage.

So, at sixteen, I was wise beyond my years, from taking responsibility helping my Mum and dad bring up the kids. I often provided emotional support to both my mum and dad who had a tempestuous relationship especially in the first half of their marriage. Money was quite tight, another reason why I knew instinctively that I had no option but to leave school and obtain gainful employment at sixteen.

I don't blame mum and dad; it was simply how it was. I was brought up in a working-class family, both my parents worked, my mum had a variety of full and part time jobs to support the family and my dad worked initially as a Coal Miner and ended his working life on the 'magic eye' counting beans at Heinz.

I consider an additional contributing factor to be, that it simply was not expected that I would go to college or university. There was little evidence of any of my relatives having attended college, aside from my eldest cousin on the paternal side, staying on to 6th form doing A levels, clever bugger! I don't think Education was really valued back then.

There was no drama if I failed to do homework or had a day or two off school. I probably wagged 4/5 days a week by the time I was in 5th form in favour of working, and I eventually failed seven out of ten of my GCEs. I don't have many regrets in life, but an important one is, that I regret not listening at school.

So, after breezing/blagging my way through Notre Dame high school whilst working at many part-time roles, I was fortunate to apply for two jobs and be successful in being offered both. This was an enviable position to be in in 1974. I was after all pretty streetwise, I already had a couple of years part-time work under my belt as I previously mentioned, Saturday girl at the Co-Op Cafe and Monday to Friday girl at the Whitesmith.

Fortunately, my street wisdom stood me in good stead, I recognise that I'm blest, fortunate to have had what I consider a great life in general and a successful working life.

It didn't happen by accident, as my mum used to say "you don't get out for nowt ", and she was right. I mainly went the long way round so I flunked my 'O' levels at the best Catholic girl's grammar school in Wigan, and in order to get ahead I had to re-study and re-sit them two years later at 'night school' school... what a dunce! Mind you, even back forty-six years ago, it didn't take me long to discover that once I get on track, I'm pretty awesome.

So going back to my two job offers.

My first one was from Great Universal Stores, affectionately known as GUS locally. Everyone who was anyone worked at GUS. Their selling platform was a thick catalogue of a myriad of wonderful items, affordable, because you could buy them "on tick'. The 1970s was a time when the catalogue business was booming, most women "ran a catalogue". It was the precursor to online shopping. There has almost been a full circle since then, difference between a catalogue and a screen to get your mail order goods.

The woman who "ran the catalogue", would take the orders, deliver their goods ordered by their friends and family then collect weekly payments. In turn they earned commission on the payments and discount on their own orders.

Second offer was a clerk with the local education authority of Wigan Council. I jumped at the offer of working for the local authority and started my job working in the student grant department, Further Education or FE as it was affectionately known.

Thus in 1974, I became a wage slave. Having started work I also became a purposeful, useful member of society.

I continued working hard to keep all my plates spinning between my paid employment and practical contributions to bringing up the kids. It soon became apparent that when I started work, my real learning began.

Sixteen was also about the time I became interested in boys... and there were plenty to choose from. Having attended an all-girls grammar school, it was about time I invested some of my time in learning and developing my relationship skills. "Two timing" boys was a skill of mine, I would meet one at 7 and another at 9 ... phew! I was a much sought-after piece of eye candy back then in my hot pants!

The local fishwives soon jumped on the new gossip topic and quickly concluded that ... "You'll see where she'll end up" Little did they know that at "The Convent", our only lesson in sex Education was a book called "My Dearest Daughter" taught by Sister Pat in Biology, who talked more about the birds than the bees, if you get my drift. Mum and dad were no more forthcoming, so it was pretty much in the imagination.

My dad had a good sense of humour though, and had appointed my little sister Michelle, chief bodyguard, always ensuring that the "not getting pregnant" part of the deal was fulfilled by my little chaperone, to ensure there was no funny business and, I have to say ... it worked a treat. The downside of course was that boys started giving me a wide berth when I had Michelle in tow.

So, in July of 1974, I started my Further Education, in Further Education. My street cred with the local gossips improved significantly when I became a "civil servant". I can't describe the pleasure I felt hearing my mum telling her pal ...

"Oh yes, she's got a very good job with the council now she's left school, I always knew she would do well" ...

Ha! I think mum even developed a "telephone voice" when we came up in the world.

My salary was £80 a month, my first wage packet treated my mum to a tumble dryer, she thought she was the bee's knees. There definitely was a lot to be said for keeping up with the Fish Wives.

I was on the lowest rung of the ladder and the only way was up. Clerical 1 equalled the post opener, coffee fetcher, filing clerk, gopher, delivery girl, errand girl.

I felt extremely important sat in the Director of Education's conference room opening post, tittle tattling with the hoy poloy! Mona, the Director's secretary and I had some very interesting conversations, she was an extremely 'posh' woman, dressed from head to toe in Jaeger and very dainty kitten heel shoes. She was my 'go to' person for advice on meetings & conference room etiquette. I was able to observe conversations between various Directors/ Assistants / Advisors. It was an "Education" in itself, I learned to read lips and body language which was the beginning of my communications skills learning ... Lol

Having developed my own telephone voice, I was soon answering the phones and fitting in very well thank you. In those days, you looked at your colleague opposite through a fog of silk cut smoke, most desks had overflowed ashtrays and a tower of plastic coffee cups by 5pm, and I loved it with a passion.

Boy, did I learn a lot! There was an active branch of the Local Government trade union, NALGO and I quickly became involved as Secretary of the Young Members committee, my first experience of committee life. With it, came excursions to conference rubbing shoulders with some famous faces. All night parties in the Adelphi Hotel in Liverpool or the Queens on Blackpool prom at the annual conference. One of my claims to fame is that at one of the said conferences, I shared a breakfast table with a guy called Andy Bevan, the grandson of the founder of the NHS, Aneurin Bevan. Affectionately known as Nye, he was the deputy leader of the Labour Party in Clement Attlee's Government and Minister for Health after the Second World War. Nye Bevan led the establishment of the National Health Service. I dined out on the Andy Bevan meeting in the late 1980s whilst training to be a Health Visitor at UCLAN in Preston. The social policy lecturer was most impressed!

I became accustomed to other "meetings" too. As coffee gopher, I would frequently walk the corridors of power with my little coffee tray down to the basement machine for 6 x 1p cups of coffee. I quickly cottoned on to the informal (nod nod, wink, wink) meetings on the back stairs where doe eyed clerks looked intensely into the eyes of Assistant Directors and Advisors. Clutching clipboards and files to show they were sticking to the 'Agenda", it was comedy gold seeing them shift about as I approached and asked if they wanted a coffee...

I also learned just how naive I was, one Monday morning I was deployed to man the reception desk in the foyer, directing members of the public to different departments. I felt so important, I was buzzing. There I was in my navy-blue trouser suit like Lady Muck reigning over my little empire. Things couldn't, in my sixteen-year-old mind, get much better.

Then about 11am, two guys in overalls walked up to the desk and greeted me ...

"Hello love, we've come for the desk".
Ummm, I thought, "Where you from boys?"
"Works department, were taking it to be repaired, the drawers are a bit dodgy, you can phone the department if you want."
"No, no, it's OK" I reassured them, well after all I was in charge. So, without further ado, I collected my files and strolled back to the office.

It wasn't until the afternoon; I got a call from the Director of Education asking me where the desk was? It was like a call from God... apparently the student's union from the local College had "kidnapped" the desk as part of Rag week and had phoned to demand a ransom I think they were demanding a fiver or off with its legs ...

I made many long-lasting friendships in my maiden opening at "Wigan Metro" and I owe many of my organisational and admin skills to that role, as well as ... coffee making and spotting illicit affairs My Metro career lasted 4 years, I was getting itchy feet and a yearning for progression. There had been a major re-organisation of the Local Authority shortly before I started in 74 and promotion was limited.

Fortunately for me, dad had bought the Evening Post, I saw an advert for pupil nurses at Billinge Hospital and without further ado, I sent in my application. I didn't tell my mum and dad till I was invited for an interview, then the shit hit the fan. My dad's conclusion to my successful recruitment into nursing was "You'll never make a nurse as long as you've a hole in your ass" He was a card! So, in May 1978, I donned my nurses' hat, starched apron and set about saving lives...

Had dad not bought the Post, and had I stuck at it, maybe I could have ended up Director of Education.

Chapter 9

To Billinge & Beyond

At twenty-one years old, eyes set on a nursing career, I left my weekday jobs and 9-5. I was excited to be starting nurse training at Billinge Hospital, even though it meant a drop in pay. My dad thought I'd gone completely out of my mind and was still of the opinion that I'd never make a nurse!

My grandad had greater faith in me, he even volunteered to be my guinea pig if I wanted someone to practice injections on and advanced me a £100 loan to buy my first motorbike, so that I could get to the hospital for my shifts at Billinge.

He was amazing, a great role model, and one of my best friends. I was now the proud owner of a moped, it provided a laugh a minute as I frantically turned the pedals to get the engine to spark up but have wheels will travel as they say. It also started my second love affair ... with Motorbikes.

More importantly, it proved to be one of the primary lessons in my life, and grandad knew it. I agreed to pay back my loan at a rate of £10 per month. I placed great importance on not letting him down and on payday, withdrew the £10 first payment of my loan, money in hand, I went to see him to make payment.

"Well, I'm impressed love, he remarked" and slipped the tenner into his wallet. After three prompt payments, he sat me down and explained,

"I'm so glad, I afforded you this loan love. I want to tell you that, as you have shown you can keep your side of the bargain, you need not make any further payments. I've wiped the slate clean. I'm proud that you've decided to train to be a nurse and I want you to know, I'm here to help you where I can."

Ironically eighteen months later, he passed away in the hospital where I was training. It was one of the saddest days of my life.

I started my training on the 8th of May 1978 at The Wigan Area School of Nursing at the Elms at Wigan Infirmary. I'll never forget it as long as I live. I was bursting with pride when I put on my uniform for the first time. Pale blue dress, red belt and one out of a pile of white starched aprons. Oh, and not to forget a nurses cap Recollection of those days makes me feel "fuzzy" inside. It was apparent from the first day that being a nurse was a privileged position, the tutors demanded a certain air of respect, and woe betide anyone who allowed the standards to slip! It was quite clear that when

wearing that uniform, people expected a certain standard of behaviour.

I had moved from a very male dominated working environment and done a complete 360 into a matriarchal, female domain. I feel that my four years' experience stood me in great stead for what was to come.

Working in Education had been a good learning experience, taught me basic organisational and clerical skills, more importantly working relationship skills. I had also developed a sense of justice and the need for fairness through my work with the Trade Union NALGO. I consider myself fortunate at this early age to have met influential people and good role models. Approaching my Nursing career with a fair few inbuilt principles gave me a head start.

Training school consisted of an initial eight week that was called PTS in "school" then 8-week placements on various wards and departments to gain a varied experience and knowledge. I was part of the Billinge

Hospital "family", that's what it felt like. Sadly, the hospital site has long since been demolished and replaced with a fancy housing estate.

I was allocated my first placement on a ward for the elderly G2, a very vivid memory. I still remember the first qualified nurse I worked with; her name was Edna. Just about 10 minutes into my first shift, as I was trailing Edna like a little lap dog, and she, taking everything in her stride, whispered to me that our first job of the morning was bathing and preparing a patient who had passed away, for transfer to "Rose Cottage". I had never seen a dead body before, frightened was not the word.

Looking back, Edna was a great role model, she led by example. Even to this day I remember the respect she showed to her patient that first morning, even whilst having responsibility for teaching me as well. Edna "talked" Fred all the way through every step of the procedure as if he were with us, I was never afraid again. Not just that day, but on a continuing basis Edna taught me confidence. The way she and other nurses on my first ward spoke to, treated, and responded to the patients in their care was impressive. I added the skills to my bank and moved on. G2 eventually became the ward where I was assigned my first job as Ward Sister.... Full circle.

Edna wasn't the only great role model. I loved every minute of it, I have a "Outstanding" list of colleagues who contributed to the nurse I am today. So, Edna was one of my 1st contacts in nursing on the wards and would have no idea how much she influenced me.

There are many senior members who remain close to my heart. My memories of two outstanding nurse colleagues make me smile when I think of them.

84

They were like a double act, the ward sister Irene Midgy and her enrolled nurse, affectionately known as Mac, both looked like they were off the front of the Nursing Times, each had highly polished badges pinned to the neck of their uniform, hair immaculate, tutti on.

They exuded professionalism, the pair of them. The ward was run like a military operation, all the bed counterpanes had to be so many inches turned back, lockers dusted, flowers placed precisely. Bed tables at the bottom of the bed.

The patient care was exemplary. It was a pleasure working on the ward. Their enthusiasm rubbed off on every person on the ward, it was great.

For some reason, the ward sister recognised my talent for shaving, on gynaecology, before theatre, everyone had to be shaved from "nipple to knee" and I became the barber during my placement. What a skill that was! Good job vagazzles hadn't been invented or there could have been murder. Another tip I learned from Sr Midgy was that after an abdominal operation, she would treat all her ladies in a bath containing Lux soap flakes! Worked wonders for the skin, although I should probably add a disclaimer to not try this at home, I think the Cross-infection brigade would have a field day!

I am privileged to still be friends many colleagues whom I trained with and some who were qualified well before I began.

Another longstanding friend from Billinge, Margaret O'Grady, a beautiful friend from the Emerald Isle, never ceases to make me smile. She not only guided me through some of my early years in nurse training also became an influential mentor in my Health Visiting Career. Now we're both retired, we keep in touch and meet occasionally. She probably doesn't realise the support she gave me.

I'm still a nurse inside, despite having retired twelve years ago!

It's a standing joke with my OH and the kids...

"Oh, did you not know, mum was a nurse."
"How long was it mum ... 30 years"
"Yes, she was a nurse for 30 years."

In many ways, especially since retirement, I have come to the realisation that in many situations in society, people define you by your job or status. It's usually one of the opening questions when conversing with someone you meet for the first time. Folks judge you by it, painting a first impression picture.

Whether you like it or not, people's ears prick up if you have a job, they regard as important or commanding respect. The "Don't judge a book by its cover" saying comes to mind. We all make snap judgements. I digress ...

It wasn't all plain sailing, I had many "run ins" with various figures of Authority, not least since I had my own ideas of how people should be treated. I wouldn't be me unless I stood up for what I believed in, then and now. It's especially important to me to be true to myself.

At the end of each placement, both at Billinge and Wigan Infirmary, with trepidation we would be called into the sister's office to discover our fate in the form of a "Report". Subsequently the Nursing Officer, next up the line would then be afforded the opportunity of putting her ten penneth in.

The Nursing Officer would strike fear into the heart of anyone. One in particular comes to mind, an Irish woman, let's call her Fanlight Fanny.

My mum would have described her as a "stiff, thick set woman (Bonny build and lacking a sense of humour), with blonde hair which looked as if she had a "set" at the hairdressers on rollers every Friday. She had a raucous Irish accent which had not benefited from her stay in the North of England.

Fanny wore a Royal blue skirt suit with a starched white blouse underneath and black low heeled court shoes. She had the knack of creeping / turning up on wards when you least expected it. Pupil nurses were especially filled with fear when she walked on the ward. I experienced her wrath!

On one said occasion, she caught me sat on the bed of a patient just before visiting time. He was a friendly character called Cliff, a porter in the hospital and I was simply offering him a bit of friendly reassurance. I had my back to the door, so before I knew it, she was stood at the bottom of his bed.

"Nurse!" She shouted in that inimitable Irish accent.

I must have almost jumped out of my skin, I was a 21-year-old kid, new to the job, added to which I was chewing gum. An absolute crime against Nursing! I stood to attention like a frightened squaddie.

"Not only spreading infection sat brazenly on that bed, chewing gum! ... You just remind me of a factory girl!"

My patient's face was a picture, I was instructed to accompany her on a ward round explaining the details of why each patient was in hospital as my punishment. Fortunately, I've always been a smart ass and even then, I had all the answers. Going forward, for years after, even as a ward sister, my porter friend reminded me of that day, he used to sing "Sally" by Gracie Fields every time in was in his vicinity.

I almost threw the towel in on one occasion when the Ward Sister had made a remark which I found just a bit petty.

"Nurse Maloney lacks attention to detail."

... You might have gathered, I don't suffer fools gladly!

On discussion, it was apparent that she was referring to one occasion when I had failed to remember the tape on the trolley when undertaking a dressing. She was most put out when I told her I didn't agree and would not sign it. At 22, I was probably less diplomatic than I endeavour to be now, and not being accustomed to a pupil nurse who answered back, she took great exception. I don't suppose many pupil nurses arrive with the skills of a Shop Steward in their back pocket. In any case, I was not going to be unjustly treated and she was left in no doubt.

Cutting a long story short, I left the ward scribbled my resignation, and went to hand in my notice with the Tutors office. I came face to face with my clinical nurse teacher in the corridor whilst stomping down to see her. I suggested to her that the ward sister ought to be kinder

to me on her way up as she might meet me on her way down, it still makes me smile now. She sat me down with a coffee and a cig, (everyone smoked in those days) and sorted it out with her usual diplomacy! I have on occasion bumped into that very Ward Sister, now retired, I always have a little smile to myself, God love her.
I'm glad the tutor persuaded me to stay!

My successful completion of my 2 years training and subsequent 2 years training at Wigan Infirmary saw me promoted through the ranks from Enrolled Nurse to Staff Nurse to Ward Sister.
It was at that point, dad installed a photo of me in his wallet, in my sisters' uniform. I mean I was even beginning to prove the fish wives wrong and …obviously, the hole in my ass had healed by then, Ha!

In my post as a Staff Nurse, I took great pleasure in mentoring student nurses, for me it was mutually beneficial. It was one of the most important parts of my role, I loved being hands on. Bedside nursing one to one with patients now in my care was the most rewarding thing I've ever experienced. I felt absolute empathy with them, it's an incredibly special relationship to be trusted to look after someone's nearest and dearest. Especially at their most vulnerable, it underlined the lesson of why nurses are expected to behave in an exemplary manner. I would implore nurses to remember that "The heart attack in bed 1" is someone's mother, father, sister, brother, grandma, grandad, friend etc. …

I loved the variety, teaching, mentoring, problem solving, input into patient care plans, direct involvement in hands on care. It seemed a natural progression for me to apply for the sister's post when the opportunity arose. I was absolutely delighted to be appointed and approached my newfound responsibilities with great enthusiasm. Little did I realise that I was moving out of "bedside" nursing to simply being involved in the administration of care. As Ward Sister I simply didn't have enough hands to be full on in the practical and management aspects of care. I soon found out that every doctor who walked on the ward, wanted the woman in navy blue... it had simply been the wrong move for me.

After just 6 months, I longed to be back teaching and working at the "coal face". I faced the wrath of the Nursing Officer, another stiff woman, this time a tall St Helener with blonde hair, lol, who concluded that I didn't know what I wanted, and I should make my mind up...
Without further ado and thanks to another advert in The Post, I applied to train as a Health Visitor starting in 1988. Without much hope, as I was going from looking after elderly men to new borns. With no paediatric or midwifery experience, I thought I didn't have a cat in hells chance.

With absolute delight I learned that I had been successful and had to endure an exceedingly difficult notice period. My colleagues were forbidden to mention my new job, so everyone simply ignored the fact that I was leaving. My last contact on the day I was leaving, my shift which ended at 1.15pm, was an attempt to say farewell to the Nursing Officer, who in a very dismissive tone ...
"I'll speak to **you** on Monday" she squawked ... I didn't respond.
I've never set eyes on her from that day to this ...

My ward colleagues bade me farewell and sent me on my way with a black executive briefcase.
It put a very sour end to a wonderful 10 years

Chapter 10

A Nice Little Job?

So, by 1988 both my career and my personal life had taken an upturn. I was in a steady relationship with my sweetheart and was now divorced from my X. He had turned up at my door on my birthday in 1987 and presented me with a petition for divorce, I signed up for freedom and told him, I wasn't going to complain. Looking back now, it turned out to be a lucky escape!

I had moved out of the nurse's home and bought a little house near to the Health Centre where I was based and settled into a nice life, thank you very much.

I was proud as Punch to have been successful in gaining a place at UCLAN Preston, as Student Health Visitor. You apparently needed a letter from God to get on, so quite naturally, I was glowing, it must have been the executive briefcase. Holding my head high, I quickly adjusted to wearing my halo... One of the stand-out placements of my Registered Nurse training had been with a wonderful, inspirational, Health Visitor, Patricia Hamilton at Sherwood Drive Clinic. She turned out to be a continued source of inspiration and motivation throughout my subsequent HV Career.

I had no idea just how diverse a role it would be, it was literally a case of no two days the same. I quickly came to realise that it was possible to make a real difference to people's lives, which is an absolute joy. My OH always joked it was all 'Tea and Custard Creams' The truth is, it wasn't a nice little job, it was a wonderful job, including the custard creams! Added to which I was back to 9-5 Monday to Friday.

My paternal grandad's motto was:
"If I can help somebody as I pass along, then my living has not been in vain."

After ten years in hospital nursing, my focus had to change from caring for sick patients to working to promote good health and wellbeing. Going from trying to 'fix' people to preventing them getting sick.
Not only a simply medical, but a holistic view, considering the physical, emotional, psychological, and spiritual health. Understanding how sociological and

environmental factors contribute to ill health. After all, it's no good trying to lecture to someone to eat a healthy diet if they don't have the knowledge or funds to buy healthy food.

It's a bit like looking after your car, you need to have it serviced, change the oil, top it up with water, give it fuel and don't run it into the ground.

At the start of my HV career, I was based in the suburbs, visiting families in a mixture of private and social housing, some parts affluent and some very materially deprived. The relationship of a parent and HV is to me, incredibly special. After all, they are inviting you into their home and it deserves all the respect. On first meeting, they would always 'suss' you out...
'So have you got children then?'
'Where you from?'

Initially the impression I got was that as a Health Visitor, the perception was one of the nosy woman from the health centre. HVs sadly, seemed to have a certain reputation, people were somehow under the impression that you had visited to catch them out or be the child catcher. So, the first job was breaking down the myths and barriers.

I have a very strong belief in starting with a level playing field, in my eyes, my job was to empower the parent (it was usually the mother whom I met), to be in complete control. Communication is the basis of a good relationship. Once we had got over the idea I wasn't from the posh part of town or been brought up with a silver spoon in my mouth, things usually improved.
To say I loved my job was a massive understatement, I felt privileged to be able to help parents and carers achieve their full potential. In my opinion, my role encompassed promoting the health of all the family.

There are no perfect parents, so my aim was that I should empower my clients to be 'good enough'. It does no one any favours expecting too much of themselves in the parenting game. It takes time to adjust when a child comes along, bonding, getting to know each other. Added to which, the need to empower dads to get involved. Being focused on promoting good health involved all the family, sometimes people thought the health visitor only talked to mothers. There were a few dads dropped on during the testicular cancer health promotion campaign. It's refreshing to see how the role of dads has changed over the years. I enjoyed encouraging dads taking an active part in parenting, unlike in my mum & dad's day when it was unheard of.

Contributing to the wellbeing of families with children is a rewarding and fulfilling job. I have to say, it dawned on me remarkably early, that I had been subject to a sheltered life. It was a steep learning curve working in an area of a level of deprivation where families were living under the poverty line.

There was a strong sense of community, everyone knew each other, generations of families had grown up on the estate. The rule was, if someone hurt one of them, they all bled, and the consequences rippled out through the estate. We were attached to GP practices back then, so when I visited a new mum, it was likely I had already visited her sister, aunt, and friend round the corner when they had their babies. The importance of establishing a trusting relationship was paramount as the bongo drums were very loud if there was any gossip going around. It went round the estate like wildfire.

I would drive onto the estate and park up then walk from house to house, it was a brilliant opportunity to catch up with the community as I'd bump into several of my mums, grans aunts and friends along the way. I'd find out all sorts of the local gossip of who was doing what, who was going with who and new pregnancies. Face to face is the best way of finding out all the gossip, take everything with a large pinch of salt. Not only that, but I would also be able to observe people on the estate just going about their business. Obviously as HV the news was one way, with a strong emphasis on confidentiality. With that in mind, impromptu 'visits' when I was stopped on the street for small chats, I think was sometimes instrumental in stopping big issues as mums would say "can I just ask you .... while your passing?" Someone once advised me, believe only half of what you see, and nothing that you hear and they're correct!

Some young families were housed in high rise flats 16 storeys high. What a challenge feeling safe going up and down the lifts not knowing who I would meet. It undoubtedly affected young parents being up in the sky, not seeing neighbours passing, and having no outside space. It's not surprising that post-natal depression was rife with the social isolation caused by this type of housing. I would wait for the lift doors opening and with one leg still in the lift so the doors couldn't close, I'd try to get the attention of the young woman I was visiting. Getting stranded on the 16th floor was my worst nightmare. At the time there were no mobiles, so no one knew where you were apart from what was in your diary. It took some getting used to.

We were all in the same boat when I came to our client's pets. I don't think folks realised that even though THEY loved Brutus, and thought he was 'really soft', MY heart was in my mouth, and I was full of anxiety as I knocked

on the door and there is the sound of what I imagined was a dog that would rip your leg off. On one occasion, the Grandad of the house answered the door with a rifle in his hand, and said nonchalantly...

"Come in love, I didn't realise it was you."

There is loud barking emanating from the kitchen where he's locked Brutus, and by the sounds of things, the hound would have chewed through the door in a crack. I was shown through to his newly delivered daughter, with Grandad still holding the rifle. He must have sensed the fear in my face and explained it was only an air rifle, and as Brutus took his first chunk out of the door, the new mum pointed to the kitchen door and said ...

"He's very protective of the baby!" Eeek!

It wasn't unusual to be confronted by guard dogs. I remember my friend Anita asking me to follow her onto the estate. The neighbour next to house where she was visiting had a massive dog which tried to jump the fence every time she visited. We turned up like Scott and Bailey, I was parked at the end of the drive, suicide door open on the car in case she had to make a speedy retreat chased by Rover. I remember her wearing 'sensible' shoes just in case.

Dogs were not the only pets that caused a bit of a stir for me during visits. I used to visit a lovely family who had two or three children and had a liking for bearded dragon lizards. When I would go to visit, on both sides of the chimney breast, there with these tanks filled with tropical plants and tree branches. It would be fascinating', sitting there observing, as she would go in the back and make a cup of tea (and bring the custard creams) before we sat down to chat. Whilst she was away, the bearded dragon would be stood like a statue on the branch occasionally blinking one eye.

I used to ask her about them, and she would tell me in great detail how she fed them, what she fed them on and how sometimes she would take them out of the tank and let them have a roam around. For that reason, I would always cast my eyes to make sure that the dragon was in the tank as I got there.

One particular day I arrived at the house, and I was a little distracted trying to park and never even thought about the lizard as I approached the door. Once inside, we sat down quite quickly and got on with the visit. For some reason I never checked out if Charlie was in the tank. It was quite a long visit as it was the first or primary visit after birth, and I would have to examine the baby

and take some blood samples. I was sat on the chair just inside the living room door and was focused on the job in hand. Everything went swimmingly, and just as I was packing up to leave, she said with a smile on her face,

"What's happened? you've not asked about him today, and he's been right there looking at you the whole time."

I turned my head, and sure enough sat about 6 inches from my head was Charlie, sat on the back of the armchair. He was nearly as big as that bloody Alsatian! I almost wet myself!

Running parallel to my HV career was our Launderette Business managed and run by my OH. We had bought it just after the birth of Claire our youngest daughter, and it was on my patch. I would visit at lunchtime to share a brew with my sweetheart.

Lots of our customers were gypsies and travellers, some from settled gypsy sites and some living on the roadside. Gypsy women would come into our shop with their children and having established a trusting relationship with my sweetheart would ask his advice about where to go for 'needles' (Immunisations) or simple health advice. He would tell them to come in at lunchtime and I would be there to help them, it was the start of my interest in the health of travellers. It wasn't long before I was the go-to person if there were any travellers in the area and lead to my being Specialist HV for gypsies and travellers.

It was an interesting time in my career, the culture of this ethnic minority group demanded a whole new approach, however, I had a head start. All the gypsy families knew me as 'The woman from the Wash-House", their doing business with my husband had bestowed a kind of trust in me too, a trust which most health professionals don't have with this group. It was adventurous too! I'd have to go looking in the wilds for illegal camps and in the process get chased by yappy dogs. The good thing was that the head honcho would 'call off the dogs' when he saw it was the woman from the Bag-Wash ... Lol.

I would hold an impromptu baby clinic in one of the caravans which would act as a one stop shop for everything from advice about vaccinations, weighing babies, looking at rashes, dropping off baby milk and them trying to sell me rugs and other paraphernalia. The life expectancy of this group was well below that of the settled population, simply because of their lifestyle. The number of fatal childhood accidents in the gypsy population I visited was alarming.

Working within this unique population and culture enriched my life, in some ways I 'felt' the discrimination levelled towards them. GP practice staff were sometimes wary of temporary registration, quite understandably sometimes because sometimes the traveller population didn't have the same regard/ trust and would be difficult to fit into the rules and procedures of practices. They would default on appointments for children's immunisation because for whatever reason they had to move on. This would sometimes be due to being evicted from land or private property. I would act as advocate for them and try to get people to understand their culture, but it was difficult when a GP practice had targets to meet and boxes to tick. I also had input into the Traveller Education Service to influence parents allowing their children to attend school.

Every part of my job was a challenge, it was totally engaging and rewarding, a privilege that I didn't take lightly. I was fortunate to have the opportunity to work closely with mums when I set up and managed the 'Neighbourhood Mums' project, which was a volunteer project where experienced mothers supported, new mums. It was based on a model first born in The Eastern Health Board, Southern Ireland. The benefit of the project was that it served to empower both the volunteer and mum, they learned new skills which had a mutually beneficial knock-on effect. The experienced trained volunteer would visit and mentor a new mum on a monthly basis. With the help of cartoon information sheets, they would have discussions on all sorts of health and parenting topics. Often there would be greater trust between people from the same community. The project also opened up, and provided learning and social opportunities for women involved, attending and organising conferences and courses. It was just magic!

Health Visiting perse, was an incredibly rewarding career, I spent 20 years working in the community and am proud of my achievement and thankful for the experience. The families I visited were all unique, all had their challenges like every family, including mine!

I was privileged to be invited into their homes and share their joy when their children came into the world, and their intimate thoughts and confidences. For many, our discussions were akin to watering the plants / simply nurturing & teaching, for others helping make sense of serious health and social issues. In some areas, the material deprivation was crippling but they weren't short of love and caring for their children. I'm proud that I can count times when my interaction with families has been life changing, after all, that's what life is about.

To sum it up, there are no perfect parents, although society would have you believe there are. What matters is that we are "good enough" and we are present to support our children and each other through good days and not so good days.

Chapter 11

Reflections on a former life

In what now seems like a past life, I was married for a short period in my early 20s, I look back with some fond memories which have stayed with me. It represented the time I was training to be an enrolled nurse from 1978-1980, through to 1984 when I qualified as a Staff Nurse.

I am going to speak of my experiences at the time singularly as I now regard my former husband simply as another human being, to whom I was attached at the time, we shared good times and not so good times. Where I need to, I will refer to him as my X.

The notable memories of this time were many, mainly around motorbikes, magic and a stray dog all culminating in an epiphany leading to my decision to leave.

First … motorbikes

I had progressed from my moped, put ... put... through various engine sizes and finally settled on a Honda Super-Dream 250, and it was my greatest love. Red and yellow dream machine!

I just feel a slight diversion...

OMG what I would give now with my arthritic knackered knees to be able to cock my leg over that dream machine Lol. These days, I've got all on lifting my leg, to put my knickers on! I still haven't really learned my limits. I still picture in my head, being able to do a handstand like I used to. Only the other day, I attempted to stand up onto a dining chair to reach something. I got both feet up onto the chair but couldn't take my own weight to stand up. I fell arse over tit, off the chair and landed unceremoniously on the wooden floor. Murph was upstairs so I just sat on the floor, crying, unable to get myself up. It a good job I can laugh, he told the kids that he found me crying, sat on the floor, like someone had taken my toffee.

Back to my tale...

I was working at Billinge Hospital at the time, I had adopted the spikey, come on a bike hairdo. The bonce always looked like I'd just took my lid off, saved me faffing about when I had to look the part in my uniform, like my role model Sr. Midgy!

I invested in all singing and dancing bike gear which consisted of Honda green and yellow one-piece leathers, boots, gloves and a Belstaff jacket, to be double wrapped. Topped off with a full faced helmet... with a cherry on top! When I wasn't working, saving lives, I would meet friends at motorcycle rallies all over the country, be or entertaining children with magic tricks at parties.

A rally would be organised by a group of bikers who had formed a club, usually with a humorous name. Our club was based at the Gardeners Arms in Lovers Lane Atherton, we were affectionately known as the Cloghoppers MCC.

Our annual bike rally would be in the fields behind the pub. We would have probably in the region of 100 bikers camp in their 2-man tents in the field, and we would turn the barn into the canteen, barbecue station where we would flog burgers and hot dogs.

There would be lots of drink, music, dancing and a lot of daft games. Game such as 'Crankshaft throwing', dangerous to say the least. I mean if you get hit in a wellie throwing contest, it doesn't knock your brains out. There was more than one occasion where someone would get in the way of the flying object, they would be mostly well oiled anyway and shake it off forthwith...

The worst game was Tug O War.... across the canal, OMG, it would be November, pissing with rain, slippery, and nowhere to dry off. If you were lucky and didn't get dragged in the water, you would be covered from head to toe in s**t. A lot of fun when you're early 20s having the crack.

Our 'unofficial campsite' did not have toilets either, I'll leave that one to the imagination. The posh people brought all the kit, tables, chairs and such like, state of the art camping stuff, not like our little 2-man tent.

I remember in my early biking days, between moped and touring bike, riding all the way to the Campsie Fells, just south of Glasgow. I was frozen to the bone when I got there on my little 125cc Honda, got off, positioned much like when a cowboy gets off his horse. Not the most comfortable mode of transport in the world, but nevertheless arrived safely.

I was obviously more resilient in those days especially from the cold, the rain and the wind. I was also able to judge cow pats with amazing ingenuity with or without a torch. Sleeping on a washing line if necessary, so tents in freezing cold Glasgow were a piece of cake.

For my sins, I was once refused service in a little chef restaurant on the motorway services. I worked as a staff nurse at the time, but for some reason the Little Chef manager thought I was a raging Hells Angel because I was carrying a full faced crash helmet. I was totally affronted by her. An example of direct discrimination without any reason. They were great times, so if ever you see a motorcyclist, don't make assumptions, it could be me, and I'm not as forgiving now I'm an old bird!

One of my fun pastimes was working as a children's entertainer doing children's magic shows. The magician's assistant but dafter... I absolutely loved it, mind you, you always got some smart arsed kid who could spot the trick.

I used to make my own props, and simply loved practicing tricks. I had friends who did close card magic and can honestly say its mind blowing, the skill needed to pull it off. I have been sawn in half; I have to say I was nervous, even though I knew it was a trick. If you've got a minute, go on YouTube and watch Al Goshman doing a trick called cups and balls. He's spellbinding!

A few years into married life and concentrating on my career occupied my mind. I had not really thought about a family, I was still only 23. I had always almost taken for granted that at some point we would have children, but it had never really 'come up' in discussion. In hindsight, there were people who thought I was a 'career woman' and the reason we had not embraced parenthood.

I remember one day; I was on a late shift and had walked down to the garage for a loaf. As I got there, a little 'Alsatian' looking Black and Tan dog came bounding over to me wagging his tail. To cut the story short, he followed me all the way home, and despite locking him out, he was stood on his hind legs looking through the window, barking. Eventually, I succumbed and opened the door, and the rest is history. I named him K, when I left, I couldn't take K with me to the nurse's home, he had become the child we never had but sadly had to stay with my X as part of the divorce settlement.

My father-in-law had remarked.

"I wonder if a child had followed her, would she have kept it."

I hadn't realised it at the time, but he obviously thought it was MY career getting in the way.

What was not known was, that in 1981, after a long day working on the ward, I returned home off my late shift knackered and my only plan was to have a shower and relax for the night. I remember it as if it were yesterday.

I got myself a brew and was having a minute when my X announced he wanted to talk to me. I dismissed the urgency and said just wait till I'd showered, but he insisted. This is how it went...

"Can you sit down; I need to talk to you. Before I say this, I want you to know I've thought about it thoroughly and I'm not going to change my mind. I know it might destroy our marriage and I will understand if you want to leave and be with someone else."

"I want you to know that I have decided I never want children."

I had known nothing of his deliberations. If you bear in mind, I'd gone to work believing that I was in a deliriously happy marriage with a person I would spend the rest of my life with.

I was suddenly faced with this completely bizarre announcement, especially as we had never so much as mentioned children.

A discussion ensued regarding his totally selfish decision, and the only way to describe what happened between 1981-1984 is that we developed separate lives, living in the same house in a parallel universe.

I stupidly thought he might change his mind. We never so much as had an argument about it, he was that inane! I never allowed myself to shout and scream at him, in hindsight I should have "bin-bagged" him there and then and left the bags for him to collect on the lawn! I was way too soft.

It took me 3 years to decide to leave, after I found a birthday card from his secretary in his briefcase. Simmering for 3 years, only galvanised my choice to be a mother and without further drama...

I TRADED HIM IN
FOR A NEW MOTOR BIKE IN SEPT 1984

It was to be the best decision I ever made, I was now single and free to mingle and make my own choice. I moved into the nurses home next door to the girl, Sandra, who is still my best friend. In a nutshell, in January 1985 after a few months of dancing round my bag with San in the seedy nightclubs of Wigan, I met the love of my life!

On January 1st, 1985, back on track, loved up, I started on a new journey with Murph! ♥

I had only ever seen him once or twice in the local, stood at the bar and had no idea of his name or where he lived. I used to go to the local and have a pint with my dad when I was living in a parallel universe with my X. My dad had recognised by my presence sharing many pints with dad in the local, that there was something not right with my marriage. Dad welcomed me with open arms and said if I wanted to go back home, I could.

Murph & I met at a New a Year fancy dress party at the pub, I spent most of the night in the public bar with Sandra, mum and dad. I wasn't drinking as I'd driven down from the nurse's home.

Murph was celebrating with his family and friends dressed as an Arab Sheikh. He really was tall dark and handsome, a shock of black curly hair and designer stubble.

San and I made a move early in the night around 10pm to return to the home and have a few drinks to celebrate the New Year. On my way out, I bobbed my head round into the lounge, I'd won a bottle of brandy in the fancy dress and announced an invitation if anyone wanted to join us. I hadn't really expected anyone to join us, but as I opened my car door, I turned and to my delight saw an Arab Sheik stood behind me, bottle in hand.

We acquainted ourselves with each other over more than a few drinks that night, and I was delighted that we arranged to have a second date. I felt like a giddy schoolgirl contemplating my date, I still remember thinking he wasn't going to turn up. I had filled the bath almost up to my chin with bubbles. S was cracking jokes about me scaring him off because I'd be full of wrinkles after the long soak.

I was a complete bag of nerves when he turned up in 'Fergie' his dark blue, prized Ford Escort Ghia. His love affair with Fergie was about to come to an end. We enjoyed a lovely evening at a little pub called the Red Cat, before calling for a brief drink and to buy cigarettes on the way home in the Unicorn Pub near to the home. When we walked onto the car park, there was an empty space where Fergie had been, so whilst he had gained a sweetheart for life, we never clapped eyes on Fergie again!

It was the start of an incredibly special partnership, friendship & marriage. Best thing that ever happened to me! ♥

Chapter 12

If Friends were Flowers ...

Friends sometimes hold a more significant part in your heart than those you are biologically related to.

In my opinion, connections with lifelong friends are part of the glue holds me together, I think friends are like gemstones. They all have their own beautiful qualities but because of the sentiment, relationship, meaning, they're all different.

Friend
NOUN
a person with whom one has a bond of mutual affection, typically one exclusive of sexual or family relations.

I don't want to confuse what I think friendship is, we all have social media friends and naturally, they are people who have significance in our lives. For me there's a distinct difference between face to face and social media friends. Personally, I don't allow just anyone on my Facebook, or personal Instagram. I love to keep in touch with people I have met, sometimes briefly, but all must have had some impact to connect on social media. Maybe I'm old Fashioned!

The word friend should not be bandied about or used lightly in my eyes. I'm very choosy about who become my closest friends, I know without asking, they are dependable I know that they would be there no matter what the time or need was. I would personally be there if anyone of my friends or even acquaintances asked for help whoever they are, but usually, in dire needs, people turn to one of their two or three closest. Friendship to me is a two-way street, sometimes you give and sometimes you receive and sometimes it's mutually beneficial. It doesn't hold expectations of reward.

Even though we have friendships, most of us navigate our lives on a daily day without seeing them all the time. That doesn't mean that we are no longer friends, that's friendship, like stars, sometimes you can't see them they're always there.

I feel absolutely delighted if a friend calls me after not hearing from them for six months longer. We can still catch up or share a meal or drink. That connection for me, is magic. I feel that I can 'read' their signs. They are like relatives without the biology.

Friends have the capacity to put their own issues to one side and offer mutual support to each other. They don't feel the need to dominate the conversation, rather offering a listening ear.

There have been plenty of people in my life who have had a double role, many of my closest relatives have been great friends to me. My grandparents, aunts, uncles, cousins, to name a few.

I am fortunate to be part of collective friendship groups and proud especially to be a member of the worldwide profession of nurses. My best friend also belongs to this group and is like my sister. It's true to say, I've met nurses from all over the world and even people I meet for the first time have a certain respect and love for each other, we share values, experiences, and philosophy. Providing a sense of belonging and support, I am lucky to be part of it.

Without a doubt, my sweetheart, John is my best friend on a daily basis, thankfully we have had each other not only through the pandemic but for the past 36 years. We laugh daily and our relationship has had and continues to have a profound effect on my life.

We both have our little foibles but have learned to laugh. We are quite different, like chalk and cheese, but go around like a Tractor and Trailer, each taking turns at driving the tractor. He's so laid back, he's horizontal whilst I'm worrying for the world, he can't understand what is to worry about... I smile and joke that I'm his secretary, cook, lover, girlfriend, wife, cleaner, personal shopper, accountant, organiser....

I tell him I love him, and he smiles, raises his eyes and gives a cute look and says:
'I don't blame ya!"
I ask if he loves me, and he laughs and says...
"I let you look after my money don't a?"

I know he loves me and that's what counts, our relationship has spanned 36 years, so I can safely say, he's the one!

He knows exactly which buttons to press, and when, and can deliver a witty answer to most questions. Only he can come up with such daft answers. He'll crack off laughing out of the blue and when I ask him what he's laughing at, he has usually been reminded of a funny story from way back when he worked in the building trade. We will both end up in pleats laughing!

Of course, we don't always agree, in fact daily! We debate, usually not on the same page or singing from the same hymn sheet. Thankfully, each of us can take a step back... well usually me to be honest, agreeing to differ!

The relationship with your partner / husband / wife is an intimate connection which comes from knowing you have a special person in your life providing emotional support & encouragement. When you have a strong connection within your family everyone supporting each other, it provides the building blocks for future and other relationships. I felt this connection as a child growing up within a tight knit family and it has enabled me to confidently make relationships into adulthood.

Research shows that this type of support promotes good mental and physical health.

I want to share with you how my many friendships have enriched my life and continue to be a source of great joy.

I have a very special friendship with an incredible lady, spanning 18 years. This lady is selfless, humble and puts everyone before herself. Even if she hadn't had 1 minute for herself, she would give you her last 50 seconds, her last penny and her last breath all rolled into one. She does not recognise or realise just how much her friendship means to me despite reassuring her. I can honestly say she's a diamond of the highest order.

In her life, all her plates are spinning 24/7, she's a wonderfully dedicated daughter, mum, and wife, but can always find time to do a good deed. They say if you want something doing, ask someone who's busy, well that's her. I can talk to her about anything, she never judges or adds her 'two penneth' and always has value to add to any conversation.

We have a knack of understanding each other and even if there's something we don't 'get', we try to understand without jumping to judgement.

During the pandemic, we've caught up on what's App, and on one occasion, I sensed she was putting on a brave face. I thought about what might cheer her up, so I made a trip to the cake shop, bought a box of cakes and wrote a note 'I thought you were looking in need of a hug in a box' and left it on her doorstep as she needed to shield. Her little face was a picture, simple connection...I love her like a sister!

My Childhood Friend was Alison, I have a picture of her on my bedside, we met at Notre Dame High School, she was an infectious character.

She had a wonderful smile and long golden blonde hair. Ali was from Chorley, had a completely different lifestyle, she hailed from quite a well-off family. Despite our different upbringing, she and I were bosom pals.

We hit it off immediately, Alison was polar opposite to me when it came to learning. She was studious and attentive in class and always got top marks. She was like my 'Hooray Henrietta', someone I aspired to especially as she was allowed to go to nightclubs at the weekend. She would tell me tales of dancing the night away in Ribchester, I would be in awe. She was allowed to have a boyfriend...officially!

In the early Notre Dame years, Alison and I would share weekends, going and staying over in Harrison Road Chorley was heaven. She had an older brother Jeff and sister Gill at university. I was dead impressed that there was someone clever enough to go to Uni ... lol. I always knew that she was destined for greatness. When I left school having failed most of my GCEs, Alison progressed to 6th form college and university. We loosely kept in touch; she had a son when she was quite young. Our last contact found her living in the Midlands with her son and was a PA to a company director.

It was around the birth of our youngest daughter Claire in 1991. She made a special trip to visit me. I still remember that wonderful afternoon we shared. It makes me smile because, she was glamorous, as usual. I was a week after delivery, still not got it together to be able to look good and breastfeed at the same time. I liken her to Marjorie Majors in the film Shirley Valentine, with me being Shirley. I felt honoured that she'd taken time out to see me and we talked about old times. She spoke to me sincerely and naturally; she saw things very differently to me. I remember being shocked when she responded enthusiastically listening to my life experiences to date. My memories of that day are vivid and I'm blest that I had time with her. I wish I'd discovered then that you should treat each meeting as though its your last ....

We made a vow to keep in touch but for whatever reason at the time, after one or two phone calls, we lost touch again. When I was approaching my 40th birthday, I made a concerted effort to get her along to share my birthday celebrations. I had a dig around and finally contacted her brother who still lived at the house where she was brought up. It came as a massive shock to discover that she had died from ovarian cancer shortly after she visited me aged 34. I still think of her and wish I had made more time.

I have recently reconnected with my very old friend Yvonne from primary school. We were bosom buddies all through our early days at St Cuthbert's RC Primary school in Pemberton. We used to have 'sleepovers' at each other's houses all the time. I used to love going away to Green hey ... just up the road. She still looks the same as I remember way back when, with her blonde hair with red tones. We lost contact when it came to the 11 plus, I remember being gutted at the time because we ended up at different schools, then we 'bumped into each other' in Majorca 28 years ago. In recent weeks, we have met again, briefly, she still has the same lovely smile! Hopefully we will meet again soon for another catch up!

My oldest female pal of 44 years ... (from St Helens), the most amazing person, a Gemini like myself, she exudes kindness, she's gentle and affectionate. I feel love just writing about her. When we meet, it usually ends up being a very messy, few drinks and endless laughter. She was with me the night I met John.

We met whilst nursing, becoming friends after developing mutual respect as colleagues. She's what a Wiganer would call a 'beltin' nurse, even though she's

119

from St Helens! You know what they say, we all have our little foibles/ crosses to bear.

She's the girl I used to 'dance round my handbag with' in Scott's nightclub in town. We lived together in the nurse's home; our rooms joined by a corridor to what would not be termed a 'Jack n Jill bathroom'. We shared a lot of mutual hangovers too, and still do! I had a fridge in my room, so San would often come through in the morning clattering the cups in the sink disturbing my beauty sleep.

When we were out clubbing, she and I would suss out the talent. One guy in particular, comes to mind, we called him Mr. Len, he was a carpet fitter and had a distinct look of Burt Lancaster. He was a cheeky Chappy, really snappy dresser with a veritable book of chat up lines...
Sandra and I used to howl laughing at the innuendos...

'Good evening madam, would you like to see my underlay?'
'Would you like plating in the doorway and stripping round the edges?'
'Do you like your shag ... pile, long or short?' Lol!

We always went home together, after queueing in the kebab shop. Everyone in the shop would be entertained by her banter. She commanded the queue like an accomplished comedian on stage, engaging in the crack with all n sundry, and her usual line at the end of the food order would be,

"Ey...love, have ya got any bones fert dog?'

I remember a particular night when she decided she wanted fish n chips and had the taxi driver driving round trying to find a chippy.

She's a quick witted, polished communicator and a seriously good storyteller. Her tales have me rolling over. Conversely, we can exchange ideas in an intellectual and serious debate. I'm always confident that she has a balanced view and would take her advice any day of the week. I was with her the night my dad passed away. I got a call that I should go home as he had taken a turn for the worst, and without hesitation, she came with me and was at my side till the early hours. I love her like a sister.

Another lifetime friend, he is like a brother to me, also a Gemini, just 10 days my senior. We clicked from the off, almost 42 years ago, he was a colleague in the NHS. He stands out in the crowd, having the funniest laugh ever. When he rocked up for the ward round in his tweed, I'd whisper to him like 'who dressed ya" then straighten his tie and make him presentable. He still reminds me of the incredibly young man he was when we met. If you were ill, this is the Dr you would want to look after you, he has an amazing personal manner with people, he's clever and always had the greatest dedication and regard for the patients in his care.

As a friend, he is loyal, kind and his friendship is for life. I can always count on him. I remember him coming to visit me at mum and dads one Christmas Time on his way back from his sister's house. It was traditional for dad to go to the pub at lunchtime for a few pints on a weekend. A arrived whilst dad was out and settled himself on the shoes off, feet up. Mum was delighted my Dr friend was visiting and was careful not to drop any H's.

We were having a quiet chat, mum cooking dinner, when dad arrived back from the pub.

As I introduced him, dad took the reins ..
"Hello Alastair, I've heard a lot about ya lad, have ya gorra girlfriend?"
"Err no, not just now Mr Maloney."
"So are ya Gay?"
How embarrassing, but he took it all in good spirits, thank The Lord!

In the mid-80s when I separated from my husband, he was there for me, we enjoyed great times at concerts and theatres, following our shared love of live shows. He's brilliant company and a brilliant friend. We never established any romantic involvement; I don't think it was ever an issue. I was delighted when he met and married the love of his life, and they had their family. I'm proud to still be in touch with him albeit by phone.

When my mum passed away, at her funeral, he appeared out of the blue, having travelled from East Yorkshire. I was so touched; it meant a great deal to me. To me, that is the sign of a true friend.
Every time we speak, he makes me smile, only recently he announced he had discovered the series 'Happy Valley'. He was itching to tell me that the principal character played by Sarah Lancashire just reminded him of me!
"She's you in a Police Uniform!"
He went on to say ...
"Well, she's gobby, says it like it is."
He must have sensed my sharp intake of breath...
"No, I mean I really like her, she reminds me of you Denise, it's a compliment!" Lol

Last but by no means least, my brother-in-law. He and my sister are divorced but ...I didn't divorce him, I held onto him in the way a loyal sister-in-law should. He's a little gem of the highest order, a sensitive, loving brother who always thinks of everyone.

I can guarantee that if I've been feeling down or unwell, he will always make the effort to call me.

We always have a great laugh, we share a sense of humour, he has a knack of pulling faces as he speaks, he's brilliant!

He absolutely is amongst the people I call my close friends, he's a person I share my very private thoughts with total confidence. Very funny, good company, and a great shopping companion. If you want an honest opinion, somebody who can judge if something suits you, he's your man. Added to which he's creative and extremely talented with an exceptional eye for style.

I would give him my last penny whether he needed it or not. He is the one I would ask relationship advice from as he is astute, considerate, kind and non-judgmental.

One of the only people in the world I would truly trust with all my heart, I'd give him my last Rolo.

Being blest to be meeting new friends in recent years, I have developed new connections, ironically again from St Helens. We connected in Tenerife, and she is a similar soul to me. We share the same beliefs; we speak the same language. We have developed an understanding of each other already. We laugh together and can sense each other. It is an evolving friendship, one which I feel will be long lasting. Fee surprises me with her intuition and caring.

On reflection, I'm very lucky to have such a number of close connections and extremely lucky to have the ability to communicate with people. I always try to see the good in folks, it is the easiest job in the world being a critic, so I believe if you haven't got anything good to say, then keep shtum !

On reflection, I'm very lucky there is an innate relational connectedness with all my close friends, I certainly benefit from them being part of my life and I'm confident that they benefit in a similar way. It's when you feel good about spending time with each other and contribute positivity mutually. I also feel a certain aura around my friends, we share good energy and experiences.

It is very important to invest in the quality of friendships and be aware of how they provide strong ties with trustworthy people. A true friend can give you honest feedback and appraisal, help you with constructive criticism. The emotional support offered shows you that you're not alone. The essence of being lucky to have a true friend is that although you can't always see them, they are always there.

Have a think about your own connections and how they enrich your life.

Chapter 13

Fulfilling the Motherhood Person Specification

On motherhood, I had always had in my mind that one day I'd be a mum, just not really had an idea of when. Learning from the best, if I'd had to apply, I had an impressive CV... I thought!

My own mum was exceptional at her job. If you imagine a garden, I was well fed and watered, kept in a good environment. Not so much that I got bogged down, and couldn't function without her, but always knew that if needed we could call on her. She helped me make my own choices but didn't kick off if I made wrong choices or decisions. She gave respect where it was due and let me know there were boundaries. Like sheep in a field, I knew where the fence was. On top of which, she taught me to have a good sense of humour, especially in her relationship with dad! She used to come out with some corkers...

'Your father... swim?"
"He ties his braces to the tap when he's having a wash."
"He's got bad legs; they won't walk past pubs."
"Face like a farmers arse"

Don't get me wrong, she was no pushover, I didn't get all my own way and a bag to put it in.

I remember as a teenager being sat at the table having tea. I started arguing with her and before I knew it, she had thrown the wet dishcloth across the table and slapped me right in the gob (as she would have said).

I had the greatest respect for my mum and dad. No parent is perfect. It's not the same 'respect' in the new order. The aim should be, to be 'good enough'.

Can you imagine before conceiving, you had to have a job interview...?

Can you give examples of when someone has been totally dependent on you for at least 16 years, possibly longer?

Are you an effective time manager able to juggle several tasks at once?

Are you a skilled negotiator, able to be objective with a person you always put before yourself?

Do you have the patience of a saint?

Can you put puzzles together and toys that require building?

Do you have the capacity and capability to earn enough money to support another person for at least 18 years probably longer?

Are you the oracle, who knows everything including modern languages and mathematics?

Do you have teaching skills?

Have you done a counselling course?

Any mentoring experiences?

Are you Superwoman?

Endless skills and requirements

These days, with the high incidence of separation and divorce, there are many children are brought up in reconstituted or blended families. Traditionally there has been a picture of the 'wicked stepmother' portrayed in fairy tales, but children make successful bonds with many people throughout their lives.

It still doesn't make becoming parent to children who are not biologically yours easy. No matter how cute they are!

I'm not sure I would have done a better job if I had been on the 'Being a Great Step-In Mum' course. Maybe my kids have a different view but that's how I see it. I've never seen myself as a step mum, rather a "Step-In" mum, because my children, are my children. I stepped into their family which consisted of their dad (my sweetheart) and them. It must have been at least a bit daunting that their dad was holding hands with a woman they hadn't seen before. In 1991 we were blest with our youngest daughter which fulfilled my dreams to become not only a Step-in Mum but a biological one too!

John is a great dad, the tall, dark, handsome chap I fell for, was already a full-time dad when we met. So, he came as a pack of two, one and two halves! A gorgeous little 'mini me' son Martin and a beautiful dark haired little daughter Jayne with eyes and a smile to die for. Aged two and three, they were a delight! Then they grew up... no, I'm joking! Not knowing how our relationship would pan out, we took it slowly, getting to know each other.

Anyone Who knows me will know that I take my responsibilities seriously. I am not a person to treat things lightly, I give 110% to everything I do, so this especially important to me. Kid's reactions can be very different and unpredictable at best, and absolutely crazy at worst. Children say it as it is, warts and all. I think it was probably about five or six months into a relationship when I was introduced to them.
We went out for a pub lunch one Sunday. I was a bag of nerves when my sweetheart picked me up. My now sister & brother-in-law we're meeting us with the kids. When I look back on the whole event, the most striking memory was that I was wearing the most horrific bright pink fluffy cardigan. On reflection I think ... whoever dressed me? I

looked like a giant pink Puffa-lump. My mind was working overtime...

What if they hated me?

Would our romance be off if the kids didn't approve?

I had to be on my best behaviour (in my mind)

Thankfully I made a reasonable impression, the pink fluffy cardigan went down very well especially with my new little friends, so with my first interview over, I breathed a big sigh of relief.

No one tells you that it's not expected that you fall in love immediately with your sweethearts' children, it's like a new friendship, it develops, and mutual respect comes later, if you're lucky!

For me, I count myself to be in that category, in this life you never get owt for nowt as mum would say. My feeling is that as a step-in parent whether mum or dad, you must be the adult and sometimes make allowances and exceptions. If you're trying to establish a meaningful relationship with a child, it's essential to get down to their level. Understanding a kid's point of view or stepping into their shoes to see how they view things is an art.

There must be compromise and allowances made on both sides. It's an amazing journey stepping into being someone's mum, a journey I would not have missed. One thing on my mind was that I couldn't possibly take the place of their biological mum, and neither would I have wanted to. Only they could decide what their views would be as they got old enough to decide. I definitely did not want to influence their choices about it, I didn't feel it was my 'place'.

I luckily managed to develop a great relationship with their maternal grandparents, I would often accompany them to visit. In the process, I gained another set of In-Laws, sadly their grandad died but I still have regular contact with Nan whom I love to the very bones!

There were many stand out moments that make me laugh even now. I don't suppose my kids remember, but as the sentimental old bird I am, I do! Once I moved out of the nurse's home and into my little house, it was an exciting prospect having John stay over with the kids at the weekend. They would turn up in his blue Bedford Midi van, it was the start of my transition from dad's girlfriend .... to mum. It would be six years before we lived together as a family.

During those early years, we spent weekends and holidays together but during the week, their mainstays were my in-laws whom they all lived with. They were wonderful people, Mary & Jack Fedigan, sadly, both passed away now. We had great times, a slow transition.

I remember being caught 'off guard' one Saturday evening as I was getting out of the bath. Little daddy's girl came upstairs for the bathroom, and I just called to her to come in. Well, it had never been something I'd thought about... nudity, till she ran back onto the landing and shouted...

'Dad, she's got fur!'

I nearly fell over laughing, then realised she'd probably never seen a naked woman, I just brushed it off and carried on.... like ya do. She still makes me smile with stuff she comes out with now, 36 years later, and has blest us with two gorgeous grandchildren.

Once we were spending weekends together, we would be sat next to each other on the settee, and she would climb up nestling between us and look into my eyes and say...

'That's my dad'

I would laugh and reply...

'That's my boyfriend.'

She used to look at me, then as if the penny had dropped, she would smile, I think she got the joke!

She dropped another corker one day at Primary school. We had gone to wave her off on a school trip and as all the children got on the coach, we saw her talking to one of the parent helpers, her friend's mum Pat. She was chatting and pointing to us, Pat was nodding knowingly.

Off they went all waving happily, I never thought another thing about the conversation she may have been having. It was only later that I saw Pat and the issue came up. Pat was howling laughing, at the time, Jayne called her grandma 'mum', so the conversation went something like this...

Pat... "Who's that with your dad love?"
"Well, that's Denise, dad's girlfriend, we live with mum in the week and with dad's girlfriend at the weekend" Lol!

Good job Pat knew which mum she was referring to!

Little mini me, number 1 son was just a year older, a quieter character when he was an infant, bust out a bit as he got older, completely overtook himself when he was a teenager! He gets quite shirty when I tell tales about his youth ... as he has mellowed considerably to where he is now, almost 40!

I got a call from St Peter's High School one afternoon during the time when the young people were preparing for confirmation.

"Hello Mrs. Fedigan, Mrs. Kay here."

Mrs. Kay was Martin's head of year.

"As you know, we have been preparing for confirmation, well .... I wanted to let you know the name Martin has chosen."

For anyone not familiar with Christian confirmation, every candidate chooses a "confirmation" name which is usually a Saint's name. Mrs. Kay, sheepishly went on ...

"Well, he's chosen the name Judas"

He must have been the only kid in the world to choose the name of the disciple who betrayed the Lord! I could imagine the looks from his paternal gran Mary and her sister Theresa, both devout daily church attenders ... OMG!

"What do you think Mrs. Fedigan?"

I detected an air of surprise when I responded ...

"You tell him, his mum said to choose an alternative or he's going to get more than he bargained for."

The tale often comes up when we're speaking about younger days. Having recently met a new girlfriend whom we are shortly going to meet, he censured me.

"Can you leave the Judas tale till about the 5th meeting, lol" I reminded him that although he is almost 40, he will always be the child who wanted to be called Judas!

I think Martin and I, more or less got off to a good start early on, after I was a big hit making a knight fancy dress costume for him and a fluffy rabbit for little Miss.

He and his little sister were always quite competitive, especially when it came to running or swimming. As he was never very athletic, each time he lost the race, he would protest that there had been some misdemeanor on his sister's side of the line. She would laugh and run off as fast as she could with him haring behind her, not able to catch her little wiry frame. We would have to re-run the race 10 times till he won. Then he'd jump up and down cheering!

Remembering Christmas in the late 80s, for little girls, the 'in' toys were Polly Pocket, a tiny doll with an all singing and dancing house, furniture, pets etc., Cabbage Patch dolls, Oh Penny. Boys were entertained by Ghostbusters, Ninja Turtles, Rubik's cube, and some electronic games were appearing like Nintendo.

Christmas morning was always very exciting, Christmas morning '87, the kids had got up early.

"He's been!"

We could hear them downstairs. A lot of the toys required 'building', plastic houses for dolls and sets for

ghostbusters and the like. Having excitedly ripped open all the pressies Father Christmas had left, they had proceeded to open every little packet containing the various pieces to build the end product. When we got up, there was a pile of plastic 'bits' in the middle of the floor, all mixed from the various boxes!

Obviously as their 'Step-in" mum, I'd started late in the race, I never saw them as babies, or their early milestones, by the time I joined in, their little characters had been moulded. It takes longer to bond the older a child is, I think. So, on the positive side, I 'birthed' them at 2 and 3, I had a fighting chance to establish a good relationship, which I now know, I did.

It would be 6 years before we would come together and 'blended' as a family and live together full time.

That time was 1991, aged 34, to my absolute delight, I became pregnant, what they call a 'Geriatric-Primip', or older first-time mother! I moved from my little 2 bed house into what is still our home, in August 1991. The day I moved, my sweetheart and the children moved in too and we became a proper 'family'. It was a wonderful feeling for me, I was now mum to our son and daughter, and we would soon be welcoming our new baby due in November.

I can't tell you how delighted I was to be pregnant for the first time. It was the most remarkable thing ever. The most basic of human experience, that money can't buy. It was like all my birthdays at once, with Christmas and Easter thrown in, plus a lottery win! I wanted to shout it from the rooftops and must have looked like the Cheshire Cat because that's how I felt.

In my mind, looking forward to the birth of our baby easily trumps any other experience in my life, although I didn't altogether like the being pregnant feeling.

I know it sounds crazy, but I used to say to mum...
"I feel like Wimpey's have moved in."
"I'm carrying a brick."
She would laugh and joke,
"It's a boy, you're carrying all-round the front, what you going to call him?

In my mind, I secretly had wanted a daughter, but so as not to tempt fate, I avoided anything remotely like it was for a little girl, I never thought of names for a girl or even looked at dresses. My OH thought there was nothing to it, as he was a 'veteran'. I didn't tell him my thoughts, he would have poo poo'd it, definitely!

Having said that I was extremely excited, I had absolutely no idea of the joy that giving birth to our daughter would bring.

In my job, I had been privileged to be present during the birth of many beautiful babies. I had witnessed the

135

joy before but, I will never forget the experience, the bond that you have with your child within minutes of giving birth, OMG, It was love at first sight.

When I went into labour, I was blest to be looked after by 2 good friends/colleagues, so couldn't have wished for anything better. I couldn't believe when 'she' popped out, well not exactly, I was in labour 16 hours and needed a forceps delivery.

My sweetheart remembers it well, Wigan Rugby were playing Salford in the quarter finals of the Lancashire cup at The Willows. They lost 24-14! He went out to buy the 'Pink' to get the result, no internet on your phone back then, in fact … no phone! The internet became available to the public around the date we moved into our new home, 6th August 1991. That didn't mean we had it! It would quite be a few years before it was widely available.

Mum & dad were beside themselves when they heard the news, their first grandchild. Dad had retired early from work a few years earlier with a bag full of money, his 'hobby' was meeting his pals in the local almost every afternoon. I'd felt it was taking a bit of a toll on his health, so the change of focus did him a power of good and had a knock-on effect on mum too. They doted on her, I used to say to dad …

"She saved your life; you would have drunk yourself to death if she hadn't come along."

The little ones whose lives I had stepped into six years earlier were blossoming every day too. I had developed a very special love for them and while they had not been born from my womb, they were born from my heart. They were delighted with their new little sister, by this time they were 8 and 9 years old.

A vivid memory of when I came home after having her was one Sunday morning, we were having a lie in, I'd been up breast feeding during the night and we were having a lovely lie in when I heard a knock on the door. Number 1 son was downstairs and answered.

Next minute, footsteps up the stairs and our bedroom door swung open and he announced "Midwife!" She was a beautiful friendly Irish woman, added to which she was a colleague of mine. Her name was Celia. John pulled the duvet up under his chin as he was in the buff, and I imagine the last thing he needed was a friendly midwife muscling into his Sunday morning. I quickly sat up and said to her.
"Just give me a minute Celia, I'll get up."
She quickly responded with a big smile and pointed to my sweetheart...
  "You will not, he will!"
I cracked off laughing as she retreated and said, I'll be here outside. As you can imagine, it was the quickest dressing routine of the week as Murph clambered into his jogging pants and jogged off past her.

To me, mum is the person who has brought you up, who has invested time and love in your life. One of the people who would lay down their last penny and life for you. She is the person who is there for the most basic moments in life, should be first base, always on your team, your Yoda.

All my children have individually brought joy and I wouldn't be without them. They make life whole and whilst we have been through some tough times, just like any family, we always come out smiling at the end of it.

I can't believe that our older "kids" are approaching 40, that must mean I'm at least 56 ... Lol. As adults, they are our friends, we love going out with them and sharing good times both at home and away. We are fortunate to have gained another 2 sons (in law) in the process who have also enriched our family.

Our second lottery win was when we were blest with 2 lovely grandchildren ... and hopefully have not finished yet. Being a grandparent is magic, the relationship with grandchildren is totally different for me. To sum up regarding grandchildren, its like being a first-time parent all over again but with the added bonus being able to give them back. A special person whom you can spoil rotten, be their friend, make and share memories ... pure joy!

As a family, we have great gatherings, mostly involving food and drink, it's brilliant, we all get on. We laugh a lot, sometimes argue, have a few dramas, need to work together sometimes to solve a problem ... but what families don'

Think You're Past Your Best?

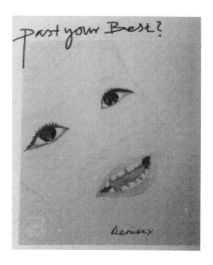

When you're getting older,
And your kids have flown the nest,
Sometimes you get the feeling
that you're past your best.
And as you quietly ponder ... if
You can fall in love once more?
The greatest gift in all the world,
Comes knocking at your door.
They are your children's children,
The rainbows of your day,
The epitome of parenthood in every single way.
Their smiles and hugs are priceless,
They make you ache with joy,
That heavenly gift from God above,
That special girl or boy!

Chapter 14

Making The Most of Life

As I'm getting older, I reflect more and more on the way I spend my time. Maybe it's only now that I have realised that time is precious, and life is too short to not make the most of each day. We mostly take for granted that we have tomorrow and hopefully we do, but always remember your part of God's queue! There's a saying, quoted by many including Eleanor Roosevelt, written by Alice Morse Earl who was an American historian and author from Massachusetts.

Yesterday is history, tomorrow's a mystery, today is a gift, that's why we call it the present.

Of your 1440 minutes a day, on average we spend 480 minutes sleeping, 450 working, 68 eating/drinking, 30 in the bathroom on hygiene and ablutions.

That leaves 412 minutes for all your other tasks, that's 6 hours & 52 minutes! Loads of time!

Obviously, it's all a bit tongue in cheek, people have so many demands on time, looking after children, school runs, cooking, cleaning, The big shop, homeschooling, helping with homework, watching Netflix and chilling, ha ha ha ha, 1,000,001 things to do and no time to do them.

So, I should start by saying I'm blest! retired, so no work demands, and I have an empty nest, so no need to feed the chicks on a daily basis. Mind you, I have to say, there is nothing quite like seeing one of your fledglings or their chicks flying back to the nest to visit, it's fabulous! It has mamma Bird preening her feathers getting ready to see them, cooking something nice to eat and getting in some treats. I don't think they quite understand just how special it is seeing them all.

One of the old sayings is, if you want something doing ask somebody who is busy. Often the busy person is organised, keeps a good diary and sets out the tasks on time in an orderly manner. If you want to get things done, it's important to schedule those tasks and set aside time to do it.

I'm that person, usually, I can't help but volunteer for everything from baking a cake to washing a camel! Added to which, I can always 'find' time! That aside, one of the important things in my opinion is to set aside 10 minutes of quiet and peace in a day.

De-clutter your mind!
To me, the world now is so full-on, 24/7 go, go, go! People never seem to stop, even when they're relaxing, it's a constant ping...message...ping...notification. It feels like everyone constantly has something to say about everything, it's a culture of nosiness!

There's nothing nicer in my mind, than taking half an hour out of the rat race, turning off all the media and just 'being."

I absolutely love getting stuck into a bit of art and can spend hours before I've realised it. It's an added bonus if doing the art is with my gorgeous granddaughter Holly, her company is great, I love our conversations and the precious quality time. It really takes me away from the hustle and bustle of the merry go round!

I also enjoy a five-minute meditation, simply sit quietly, set a 5-minute timer and focusing on breathing just clear my mind. It's amazing how refreshing it is. Try it!

I have developed an ability to accept things that happen, it is not that I don't care about things, simply I don't have control. Learning that it's not necessary to get involved in the soap operas of people's lives is refreshing. You can be in the audience without being part of the cast, that doesn't mean you can't give encouragement or support, but accepting you can't fix everything.

At the end of the day, I think most of us are aiming for a peaceful mind, and ultimate happiness.

Take Care of the little Things.

You know they say, "The devil is in the detail", well when I was a child, my Gran used to say a little ditty:

Take care of the pennies and the pounds will take care of themselves!

It was her way of letting me know that small things add up to bigger things. I have grown to understand what Gran meant.

A friend told me a little tale today about three nomads: They were traversing the desert and stopped at an oasis. After pitching their tents, a bright light appeared, and a voice told them to go out and collect pebbles and tomorrow they would be rewarded. They weren't impressed, they couldn't see the point, but as they couldn't risk taking no notice, they each went out and spent very little time collecting a few pebbles, returned to their tent and threw the pebbles into their saddle bags. They bedded down and thought no more about it.

The next day, they gave no consideration to the pebble collecting the night before till one of them went into his saddle bag. He discovered his pebbles had turned into diamonds. He shouted to his friends and celebrated his good fortune, his friends had similar good fortune. It quickly turned to disappointment when they realised had they put the effort in, they could have had so much more. One of my philosophies is "you only regret the things you didn't do.

I believe that everyone has the capacity to make a difference. In the film "It's a wonderful life" leading character George dies, and Clarence the Angel takes him back to see how much effect he has had on people's lives. You don't realise how many lives you touch when you're going about your daily business. A simple smile is a good start, it's infectious, it raises the mood when someone smiles at you. This is my rhyme called "You're Avin a Laugh

Laughter is a tonic, important every day,
It uses important muscles in a very special way,
It keeps your face from ageing, and keeps you looking good,
It spreads a lot of joy and cheer, like every human should.
So, cultivate your laughter lines, till you get bellyache,
Move your shoulders up and down, start a real earthquake.
You'll find that it's infectious, and really catches on,
And very soon the great result, life's gloominess has gone!

Be a 60-minute student.

It doesn't have to be anything mind blowing.

I learn a new word each day. I have a dictionary App which has Word of The Day. It comes up with the most remote words ever, it's really amusing, words you would think were made up...Try it!

Another little learning trick is to learn a word from another language... by the end of the week, you'll know a whole sentence!

There's no greater challenge for me than to master something new, whether it's flower arranging, pottery, growing, gardening, baking. I'm a bit of a Gill of All Trades.

I am a naturally creative person, and, on most days, you can catch me doing some sort of Blue Peter project or other. I make no apologies for it; I love learning new skills.

Usually, what happens is that someone or other is telling me about a quote they have for flowers/cakes...you name it. I then set about learning how to 'do it', I just can't resist!

Our daughter made me laugh, in 2019, she was planning her wedding and mentioned to me that she wanted a 'naked wedding cake'. I'd never heard of it, in my day, cakes were rich fruit cake. They were all singing and dancing full of intricate Royal icing and sugar flowers, dressed in their finest ball Gowns! Traditionally the top tier was saved for the christening of the first born!

Obviously, I was behind the times, I put my mind to researching into it and soon had the basics. How to

145

assemble a wedding cake? sizes, what deemed it naked? I set about making just one layer to try the icing, and abracadabra I love baking and the feeling of satisfaction at the end product.

My daughter's friend was astonished when I sent the cake to her office to share and "test it out" and asked her "How did your mum do that? My girl knows me well. Her answer made me smile.... That's my girl!

"If I asked my mum if she could tap dance.... She would be able to do it by 4pm!"

Honour the day.
As every day is special, my outlook is that it should be treated as such. I like to be the best version of me I can be, within the limitations of my ability. To me, there is every reason to be happy, seeing the sunshine coming through the blinds, even if it's a dull day, even the rain, although it might not be the weather I want today, it's good for the plants and the earth.

I also try to feel grateful for 'my lot', I acknowledge daily how blest I am, after all no one needs to look far to find someone who is worse off or in a very difficult situation. It wouldn't do me any good to have a woe is me attitude, life's hard enough without focusing on the negatives.

Always try to see the good in people and situations, if someone seems tetchy, maybe they're worried about something, maybe they don't feel well? Everyone has good and bad days. We adapt to our surroundings, simply to protect ourselves and survive.

Having endured the limitations of life under the 'C' word pandemic, we all know how quickly life can change, people can lose loved ones, life is fragile.

So, wear your best dress, put your tutti on, do your hair and nails. Eat off the best plates using the best cutlery, don't keep it for a special occasion, because today is special.

I was reading a piece by afrehlich @ www.redcross.ca
It is very poignant and true...

WE ARE THE LUCKY ONES

If you woke up this morning with more health than illness, then you are luckier than the million who will not survive this week...

If you have never experienced the danger of battle, the loneliness of imprisonment, the agony of torture, or the pangs of starvation, then you are ahead of 500 million people in the world.

If you can attend any meeting you want—political, religious, social, then you are luckier than 3 billion people in the world.

If you have food in the refrigerator, clothes on your back, a roof over your head and a place to sleep, then you are richer than 75 per cent of this world.

If you have money in the bank, in your wallet, and spare change in a dish someplace, then you are among the top eight per cent of the world's wealthy.

If you can read a list like this, then you don't belong to the 1 billion people who CANNOT read...

Help others

One of the things that I find contributes to my overall happiness is the feeling I get when I help others. I love to see the reactions of people when they receive a random act of kindness or interaction. I imagine it's like drinking the nectar of a beautiful flower when a bee calls. It fills my soul full of joy. In my opinion, that effect of giving is without a doubt as fulfilling as being on the receiving end of a good deed. Life, to me is best experienced sharing it with others, I'm a real people person.

During the 'C' word lockdown, I volunteered as a chat and check volunteer. It was so rewarding. Speaking to a total stranger might seem like a nightmare to some folks, but there's something about it that is special.

One evening about 7pm, I rang a lady, she picked up the phone and I started to introduce myself,

"Hi, I'm Denise, I'm an NHS volunteer just ringing to check if you're ok."
"Hello dear, thanks for ringing, but you're very early."
"Oh, sorry have I interrupted your programme on TV."
"No, I was asleep, it's only twenty to seven."

I realised that the lady thought it was morning, it was winter, and the night were drawing in, she was elderly and obviously lived alone. I explained to her that it was evening time. She was surprised and commented that she must have fallen asleep in her chair and that her modern TV must have turned itself off, and the night had come and caught up with her. Once she had orientated herself, we had a lovely chat, she had not seen anyone all day. The only thing I knew about her was her name then during our conversation, we were both delighted to discover that she too was a retired Health Visitor. My half hour was very well spent, in fact mutually beneficial. I said goodbye and took away a very warm feeling inside.

Connect with nature

When was the last time you connected with nature? We all go outside and travel around on the merry go round, but do we really take notice of what's around? In the good weather, I took to going for a walk with my Grand dog Poppy. Ordinarily, I wouldn't venture into the woods alone, but I felt safe with her and really enjoyed listening to nature sounds. It's amazing how shrill and beautiful the birds sound when there's nothing else polluting the background. On my way round, I would take pictures on my phone of simple little wildflowers and plants growing in the undergrowth. The most beautiful creations of nature, gorgeous colours, smells.

Taking deep breaths of the fresh air and breathing in the atmosphere makes me feel refreshed and invigorated. Just marvellous!

Chapter 15

Moving, Working and Retiring

On The Rock

I'm a firm believer in
'You only regret the things you never did.'

So, in 2008, we up sticks and moved to a rock in the Atlantic otherwise known as Tenerife. I still can't believe I did it! I took early retirement at 50, we sold our business and off we went! It was what I would call a game of two halves, 1st part all work, 2nd part all play!

We had gone there on holiday in about 1989 for the first time before having our youngest daughter. It was not a good experience; the place was inhabited by thousands of what I can only describe as human cockroaches selling time share.

They would mither the life out of us every time we stepped out of our hotel to the extent that the second week, we hardly left the accommodation. I think my OH's exact words were 'I'll never step foot in that shi* hole again!' So, the idea that we ended up there still amuses me.

We visited again around 1994 when we were royally treated to a holiday with all the family by my lovely mother-in-law Mary. We went in The Tenerife Princess hotel where the men had to dress for dinner. My OH didn't even have a pair of trousers with him and had to change into his jogging bottoms every night.

Whilst out walking one day, we happened upon a little bar, up a ginnel, a hidden oasis with a sunny terrace overlooking a swimming pool. It was heaven, run by a friendly scouser called Ritchie McGuinness & his Mrs. Cathy. They welcomed us with open arms and furnished us with lots of information about renting private apartments around the pool, I suppose the rest is history! From that day although we didn't know it at the time, we were destined for that bar.

Fast forward to October 2007 after many holidays in Marina Primavera Tenerife, we happened upon the bar owners. The lease for the bar was due to end in November the following year. To cut the story short, we struck a deal with them to buy the bar freehold and the countdown to November 2008 began.

If you had asked me in 1985 when Murph and I first met, if I would emigrate, I would have laughed till I wet myself. I was settled in a wonderful career, with three grown up kids and an adorable little grandson. I had originally thought our baby who was now 16 would come along with us, I'm not sure what I thought she would do on the holiday island but that's what was in my mind. It came as a bit of a shock when she said she didn't want to come and I still, to this day, can't believe I left her here in the UK. I mean, not exactly abandoned, our other daughter and grandson moved into our house with her.

I still remember vividly driving up the road when we leaving, I still feel the upset when I think about it, my mum and dad and the kids. I could have cried buckets, but I kept reminding myself that it was an adventure, and we could come home regularly to see them.

We left our UK home on 18th October 2008 and landed in Tenerife on 23rd after 2 ferry rides and plenty of road miles.

The ferry itself was an adventure, we bumped into two guys from Newcastle, one called Colin and one called

American Johnny who kept us amused for the three days we spent with them on the ferry.

We had a rented apartment known as 'The Villa' to stay in, it wasn't exactly that, it was more like a cave. Owned by the people we had bought the bar off, it was next door to the bar so fall out of bed into work and vice versa.

It was a very steep learning curve from the get-go. I had taken the opportunity to introduce myself to the Spanish language for two years before we moved to Tenerife. Having said that it was a slight grasp of tourist Spanish, which is not all that helpful when you have to deal with a Rottweiler from the town Hall.

I could order food and drinks in a restaurant or buy tickets in a train station but when it came to ordering propane gas for the kitchen over the phone with someone who didn't speak a word of English, it was a bit challenging! The Canarians talk at 500 mph, they love it when you try to speak Spanish, but you just say one sentence in Spanish and when they answer you, they've gone off like Speedy Gonzales.

My sweetheart only just has a grasp of English and that's Wiganese ... Lol He did learn some Spanish whilst we were there, he had to order ice over the phone, so I taught him

"Un bolso de hielo por favor"

He was extremely proud of his efforts, however once he got used to saying it, he would call the number, have the words clear in his mind.

As soon as he opened his mouth, before he could get his words out, the Spanish guy recognised his voice so would interject.... Marina Primavera? Very funny!

I remember before we moved over, I'd been learning Spanish for an academic year, and we happened to go on

154

holiday with a friend of ours. We used to like going out for trips on public transport, so this day we were out exploring and happened upon a little Spanish bar. It didn't look very touristy, but I was confident that I could communicate like a local. I told the boys to sit outside at the table on the pavement whilst I went to give the order.

The lovely Spanish barman gave me a big smile and in his best English asked me what I would like. The order rolled off my tongue in what I thought was perfect Spanish! John called to me to get some crisps, adding cheese & onion to the mix.

In no time at all, Manuel came out tray balanced with one hand at his shoulder and delivered the three beers I'd ordered, he then proceeded to go back inside. I beckoned to him had he forgotten the crisps?

"¡Si, si ... uno minuto senora! "

Minutes later, he returned with chips, cheese and onion! John chirped in...

"Well, those Spanish lessons were well worth the money!"

We had about four weeks to play with before moving into the premises. The people who were the leaseholders were at the end of their lease, it was not all that amicable with the owners who were selling to us. They were very friendly, but weren't about to help us transition, in fact when we walked into the bar after they left, there wasn't so much as a bookies pen!

We spent our first few weeks trying to find our feet, suppliers, beer companies, food companies, negotiating for furniture for the bar and dealing with the bank. It was a whole new world, in Spain when you go into the bank there is one teller there are usually 10 people queued up in front of you. The teller was slower than a tax rebate, you could easily take half a day out of your life just to go on and get some change. She would serve a couple of people, then come out from behind the desk walk past all the customers queueing up, get herself a coffee, then proceed to walk outside and have a leisurely cig whilst chatting to various people on the pavement. She made it into an art! Everyone would be chunnering and complaining.

I remember an incident when we needed some money out of the bank to buy some furniture, so one Saturday morning we turned up at the bank. It took us an hour or so to eventually get to the counter. I said in my best Spanish that we would like to withdraw €2000. The teller, a very voluptuous, glamorous Spanish woman, full face of makeup, with red lipstick outlining her pout and a very low-cut blouse looked at me and shrugged her shoulders...

"No, sorry, we have no money! "

This was a branch of the Santander bank; it was like going in the chip shop with no chips! She then very calmly said:

"Do you have a phone? give me the number and when I have your money, I will call you."

My other half and I were slightly bemused, can you imagine going in the NatWest and the counter clerk telling you that they had no money. This was only the very start of a very steep learning curve. Sure enough true to her word, about 2 hours later she rang to say, she had our money, laughable!

Quite honestly the 'Mañana' thing with the Spanish is absolutely spot on! I'm not joking when I say something that might take a month here will take 3 years on The Rock. You could describe it as any dream will do.

So, middle of November 2008 and only a month to Christmas, we became the proud owners of the "Pool Bar Marina Primavera" The previous incumbents had left behind a terrible reputation with the residents for causing a disturbance, so from day 1 we were up against it. We were oblivious to the way the complex was run and soon encountered The President, not the President of Spain as she obviously thought she was! A little gnarled Cockney who reminded me of Gollum from Lord of the Rings.

El Presidente always behaved as if we had had pissed on her chips. I don't think she had met an assertive woman before, but she was obviously feeling very threatened by my presence. It was obvious for the next 10 years. We only needed to breathe, and she was there complaining, as were all her hangers on. I told her a few times where to get off!

Between the middle of November and Christmas we managed 48 bookings for Christmas dinner. I had only ever cooked for the family before, but with my cook's hat on, we sat down and worked out a plan. We were a bit apprehensive about the arrival of what everybody was calling the Christmas family. They had been coming to the complex and bar for donkeys' years and were used to the previous owners, so with great trepidation, we went about getting ready for the influx. I recruited two unwilling volunteers Lol, our youngest daughter and her then boyfriend, to come over and lend a hand. Our other daughter was expecting our 2nd grandchild at the end of

December. Thankfully, we stood up to the test of the Christmas family and it didn't take long for them to adopt us. We had loads of volunteers, offers of help serving the Christmas lunch.

The Christmas family were something else! An utterly unique set of people who came together each year and made memories, and boy ... what memories they were. Ostrich races round he pool, blow up sumo wrestlers and wall to wall fancy dress parties. We had birthday parties, anniversary parties, they used to borrow pans from us and make scouse and curry and bring it down to the bar, everyone would muck in, it was fabulous!

Little did we know that we were in for a baptism of fire! On this beautiful island, where the sun always shines, on Christmas Eve, the heavens opened about 4pm. It rained so hard that I imagined we were going to need an ark. The bar was packed, whilst the rain was beating in through our bar shutters and flooding behind the bar.

Within a short space of time, bang! All the electricity went off and it wasn't long before we realised that the whole of Tenerife was off! Without further ado, people turned up with candles, well there was nowhere for our customers to retreat to, so next best thing, carry on drinking. The crowd were brilliant, but by the time the leccy came back on at 10.30pm, the fridges looked like a plague of locusts had been in... Empty!

However, ... the till was overflowing!

We had a mammoth 4 weeks start, between Christmas and New Year we went through 27 bottles of vodka, and a similar amount of Bacardi all washed down with hundreds of litres of Coke. Cases and cases of cider, barrels of beer, hundreds of breakfasts, lunches and dinners. By the time our guests left 1st week in January, we were knackered!

Most apartment owners were really nice, and we soon established a brisk trade. Christmas was followed by the influx of 'swallows', those lucky buggers who fly away for the Winter! An entirely different clientele, no less wonderful, happy to partake in hot pot suppers and background music and a chat till the early hours. We never went to bed the same day we got up ...

We managed to get them addicted to good Wigan/Lancashire traditions like hotpot and bacon scallops. There were plenty of our kinsfolk out for the winter too. Wiganers came from all over the island to look for us, thanks to an article in the Observer courtesy of Wendy Moss.

We became famous for roast beef barm cakes and homemade chips, hotpot suppers, and rugby league with pies at half time. We made friends with fans from every club in the league, including a few St Heleners! Pat Richards once trawled Las America's looking for us, the kids were tweeting him, he was out on holiday and asked on twitter where he could catch the match. Sadly, he didn't find us. Pleased to report many other rugby league internationals adopted the bar as their watering hole when they were over.

Each individual group of people sort of became our family so naturally we were the first point of contact for help with problems. Sadly, at least three of our guests died on the complex whilst on holiday, everyone knew each other, so all rallied round to help. I quickly learned how to deal with Spanish paramedics, police and undertakers. The bar became a venue for the wake for a lovely chap called Brian, he had been sat drinking brandy and enjoying a cigar on our terrace, the day before he died. All our customers were special to us, there were lots of real 'characters' who would relate tales and share their life experiences with us.

After a couple of years, we moved out of the Villa and rented a beautiful poolside apartment, which we bought after the owner passed away. It felt more like home, but I always knew my home was here in Blighty.

We barely had a day off in the first four years, apart from having the occasional week off to go visit home.

Crashing out on a cruise in January for a week round the Canary Islands became routine after the Christmas crowd had left, just as the swallows were arriving. I would literally be like a busted balloon, sliding down the walls I was so tired.

After four years I was starting to feel burned out with the hours, we literally never went to bed the same day we got up. There were some quieter weeks, but the rules were, we would be open till 9pm. If we had no customers at 9, we would close. We would have literally just have decided it was an early getaway, a visit to the Indian, and you could guarantee a couple of people would turn up on their way home. We would still be there having 'one for the road' at midnight. The feeling of burn out started the steady slide downhill, which everyone assumed was 'just' homesickness. There was indeed a bit of homesickness thrown into the mix.

Our granddaughter had been born on the 28th of December the first Christmas we were in Tenerife and apart from anything else, I really felt like I was missing out getting to know and establishing a bond with her. On reflection, my being in Tenerife did affect my bond with her and It's difficult to establish later on. The other draws for me were mum and dad who were both suffering deteriorating health, and I missed the kids.

Even though people pictured us "living the dream", I'm only speaking for myself when I say ... I felt that sometimes like I was in a nightmare, there was a lot of stress dealing with the community politics, always having a fight on your hands. Some owners made no secret of the fact they didn't like the bar and complained at the drop of a hat. I always felt on edge, waiting for the next thing to happen. El Presidente made it her mission to make it clear that we were not welcome on the complex, possibly she saw us as competition for her bar nearby.

My sweetheart would let it go over his head, but for me it was different. It took us 4 years to actually get our bar licence and the solicitor said it was the only one she had got through for years. Everyone runs with an 'application in process'. Our bar had been open for about 25 years, and never had a licence! Endless frustration trekking up and down to the Town Hall, visits from the Rottweiler from Health & Safety had me almost reduced to tears as he carried on that I wasn't fluent in Spanish. Being royally ripped off paying to jump through endless hoops and never knowing when the light was at the end of the tunnel, ... phew!

Into year five, we started having day off on a Monday, it would be our day when we shopped and did all the running around instead of trying to do that and work as well.

Years five and six continued to take its toll on me and what had been a great experience was turning into a drudge. We barely made it off the complex. Don't get me wrong, I enjoyed seeing people, but I'd get genuinely upset when they left, we would joke that they could stay and I would go, no one really believed that I was serious. Another issue for me was that I felt very isolated, how could that happen in a busy bar full of people all enjoying themselves laughing and joking. Looking back that was the time when I felt at my low point. I would paint on a smile and have another brandy and plan my next trip to Blighty, so I had something to look forward to. Seems a million miles away now, but when I think of that time, I still get pangs of anxiety.

My sweetheart loved the bar life, he would work 36 hours a day if need be. I was torn because I didn't want to burst his bubble, but I knew in my heart of hearts that I needed a break from the relentless merry-go-round of all work and no play. I think it almost broke his heart to sell the bar, but we were to stay and enjoy four more years in the sunshine.

In 2014 we leased our bar out and started a well-earned break. We hadn't really explored very much of the island, so it was like a breath of fresh air. It took us a month or two to get used to the freedom from long days working in the bar. We were now able to sit on the other side of the bar and enjoy the company of our loyal customers. Added to which, the stress I felt waned with every passing day.

Our house had, by this time been converted into two apartments so that we could welcome visitors to stay with us. A steady stream of people became regulars at different times of the year. I looked forward to seeing them all, some would stay a few months, they became like family. Not only that, we were also still the one stop shop for everything, we had a regular stream of visitors coming from all over. It was like a clinic, dressings, injections, advice service, booking flights agent, printing tickets, accompanying people to the Dr at the top of the road, listening to all the grumblings of the owners etc...

We had a wonderful time, I made friends with a very special person called Norma. We were similar souls, very crafty, we would meet and do what she called "Blue Peter stuff", sharing ideas about our crafting. We would meet for coffee (wine) in a local café bar and spend a few hours just chilling, chatting & watching the world go by. Also catching up with various other Ex Pats, who were also out for coffee.

We also made a considered decision that we wouldn't get into drinking seven days a week but live as we would if we were at home. We would spend our days doing the normal routine stuff, keeping the house open. We took full advantage of the beautiful views on the coast, enjoying walking for miles. There was often a quick pint thrown in just as a little incentive! We also started helping owners who were back in the UK to look after their property in their absence. On our nights out, we discovered some brilliant restaurants and became regular customers of a local Canadian restaurant, the funny thing is we didn't speak fluent Spanish, and Juan and his wife spoke no English, but we always managed to get by and end up hugging!

We would go into Adeje town, up away from the coast and enjoy the authentic Canarian spicy chicken, potatoes and salad, washed down with beautiful Mamas & Papas wine!

On one occasion accompanied by our friends Fiona & Joey, we had our fill, got slightly intoxicated, then returned to our local near home for nightcaps. We got chatting about how long we had been married, and started asking our friends the same Q. The ensuing conversation revealed that they were not in fact married but had been together longer than they cared to remember. By the end of the night, they had agreed they should get married, named the day (John's birthday) the following year and announced it on Facebook! They actually did get married on that day, but they had a lot of explaining to do the morning after the night before in Tenerife.

Tenerife is a beautiful island to explore off the beaten track with many hidden gems. Whilst travelling up and down the motorway, we had seen what looked like a glass observatory built into rock miles up into the mountain. On further investigation, we discovered it was the restaurant

"El Centinel" with an enormous panoramic window, encompassing magnificent views all over the South of Tenerife. It was one of our favourite places and would take friends and family for lunch when they visited.

We would make a round trip, first to El Centinel, then down the mountain, across the motorway to a place called "La Cueva Del Hermano Pedro" on the way to El Medano on the coast.

La Cueva is magical place, it is a little church in a cave literally at the end of the runway of Tenerife south

airport. The Cave-Shrine of Santo HermaPedro, dedicated to St Peter of St Joseph Betancur (Canary first saint). Also known as San Pedro de Vilaflor (*Saint Peter of Vilaflor*), he was also a missionary in Guatemala. Known as the "Saint Francis of Assisi of the Americas",

165

It is a tranquil oasis of calm. The atmosphere is just amazing! This cave is considered one of the most important pilgrimage spots of the Canary Islands, it is said to attract over 300.000 visitors per year, however, in the many times I have visited it has been very tranquil.

In this cave is where the saint stood with his flock to rest to recover and walk again to his small village of Vilaflor where he was born. In addition, it was also used by Peter as a place of prayer and even as a hiding place to protect himself from pirate attacks, which were abundant on the coasts of the Canary Islands at that time.

Vilaflor is the highest municipality in Spain and located high up in the Tenerife mountains. Inside the cave was a shrine to him, all manner of religious artefacts were left there, buckets of flowers covered the floor and hundreds of votive candles would be burning inside. In a separate little opening next to the main shrine is a wooden statue of St Peter and a relic which is part of one of his ribs.

Locals would be sat quietly meditating taking in the calm. Suddenly you would hear the sound of a plane approaching, taking off, then the vision flying over at what seemed like touching distance.

I have recently been thinking of another favourite place, a little village along the coast La Caleta. It's a 2.5-mile stroll along the coast, ending in the most beautiful bar Coqueluche Beach Bar, where we would while away a few hours listening to the band, watching the para gliders coming into land then the sun set.
During the pandemic, La Caleta came to my mind:

I penned a little poem called Dare to Dream ...
Dare to dream of getaways,
Of balmy weather and halcyon days,
Paragliders skimming over, just out of reach,
As the sun sets low over La Caleta beach.
As the wine glasses clink and we clap for the band,
Shadowy silhouetted lovers stroll hand in hand,
It's a million miles from Covid nineteen,
In the beautiful place where I dare to dream.

On reflection, now, amid the second year of the pandemic, I feel we were very lucky to get out when we did. Tenerife just now is dead, no tourists (or very few). I feel for friends who have bars over there, struggling to make ends meet. I think a little angel was smiling on us!

Chapter 15

You can take the Girl out of Wigan but ...

You can't take Wigan outta the Girl!

The beautiful place I call home has long been the butt of music hall jokes about its place in the smoky North of England, the pier and pies!

In reality, Wigan is full of friendly northern folk, mostly happy to help any waif and stray we come across. Everyone knows everyone in Wigan, if you stand waiting for a bus, by the time the bus comes, you'll be related to half of the queue, even if you're from miles away!

As a person, or "pie eater" as we're affectionately known, I've been blest to have had the opportunity to live in another beautiful country on the island of Tenerife.

I think if you cut me open, I'd be like a stick of rock with Wigan written all through me! Pies feature a lot in Wigan life, believe it or not the World Pie Eating Championship is held in Wigan!

Takeaway delicacies include The Wigan kebab...

4 pies on a skewer, or a pie barm, that's a pie on a bread bun to all you non-Wiganers.

Wiganers got the name "Pie Eaters" after the TUC called a general miners strike in 1926 in support of coal miners. For 9 days Britain was brought to a standstill after key workers in railways, engineering, docks, transport also downed tools to support the strike. Despite overwhelming support, the TUC were forced to back down and tell the workers to go back to work because the Government could not force employers to take back striking workers.

Miners were literally starving, but up in Wigan, the collieries had taken things into their own hands. With no food to eat, miners were forced to return to work before workers in other towns. They had become the workers who "ate humble pie". Thus, the cherished nickname pie eaters was born.

Another distinctive feature is our accent which is broad Lancashire, with a few definitive words thrown in. As a native, I can usually understand someone speaking "Lanky Twang", but not always. I used to think I'd lost my accent being away and mixing with lots of folk, but I once was needed to head a health promotion campaign speaking on the local radio. Eee By Gum! I sounded like I was definitely wearing clogs and a shawl!

I can honestly say the name of this Chapter is 100%

true. I may have looked as if I was integrating into the Spanish way of life. I could hablo the old lingo, almost like a native, but in actual fact I was a Wiganer on long stay, temporarily misplaced from the cobbles! I'm sure that my roots spread under the Atlantic, all the way to Dover and up the M6, definitely! Don't get me wrong, I loved Tenerife, our friends, our customers, but I also loved the very rare days when I heard rain on the windows, it made me feel at home. I always needed a plan for my next trip home. On 6th May 2016, on Monarch ZB565 flight to Manchester, I wrote a poem called "Leaving Paradise" to my sweetheart who had stayed behind in Tenerife.

Paradise is an island surrounded by the sea,
It's a holiday Isle for some folks.
But home to you and me.
We built our lives upon this rock,
Of sunshine sea and sand.
But as much as I love this sun-soaked isle,
My heart's in another land.
A place where friends and family live,
With friendships close at hand,
The weather in Wiggin is not that good,
But the folks are really grand.
It really fills my heart with joy,
To visit for a week or two.
But I'll always return to the paradise isle,
To my greatest love… that's you!

171

Wiganers came to the South of Tenerife in droves and would travel miles to visit us to enjoy a roast beef barm & home-made chips on our terrace, (might be a bap/ bun/ tea cake where you come from).   Word got round like wildfire! I think it's because, when you go abroad on holiday you go where you feel at home, a bit of home comfort.

We also became to go to place for Rugby League, not least because you could always guarantee to see the match, you could probably get a pie at half time too. I used to make miniature pies to hand round, I mean Rugby's not the same without a Wiggin Pie! We had fans from all over the place, we loved them all, they used to have a sweep each week during the match for 1st try and score and loads of banter! A lady called Maureen Robinson once turned up with a cutting out of the local Wigan Observer newspaper, "I've been all over looking for you two". Her husband John was a Rugby League correspondent for a National Newspaper, and she had come on a reconnaissance mission to find us. We loved it when they visited, along with many friends who had played our beloved game at a International level. We were blest with all our lovely customers from all corners of the world!

Our customers used to think I was mad, saying I'd rather be in Wigan.
I'd tell them "Sunshine every day is just as boring as rain every day" and I was serious!

Now for a bit of history...

Wigan has a population of around 320k in the whole of the Borough, which doesn't surprise me, as wherever we go in the world, we always drop on a Wiganer!

On a Canaries cruise back in 2015, we docked in Agadir, Morocco. We made it into the town on the transfer bus, a rude awakening as we saw armed guards up on the mountains overlooking the road. I'm a naturally nervous person and as we alighted the bus, we were approached by several Moroccan men wanting to give us a tour. It was incredibly unnerving. We declined and walked into the town and ended up in a Souk, the atmosphere was alive with spice. At every turn, shop owners trying to entice us to buy their wares. We snaked through what felt like a covered tunnel, there were blankets and throws keeping out the sun. As we passed one stall, there were 2 Brits who had been enticed in and were nervously drinking out of silver goblets whilst the stall holder weighed out spices into tissue bags. I averted my eyes as not to get invited in too! I held on close to my OH and put a bit of a spurt on to get out the other side. Phew...so glad to 'escape'

I took a grateful breath and thanked my lucky stars as we bagged 2 seats on the terrace of a bar adorned with a Union Jacks. We paid 10 Euros for 2 tiny bottles of beer and looked forward to returning to the ship. Just as we were finishing our drinks, the 2 Brits arrived, spices in hand, imagine the surprise when they turned out to be our friends & hosts of our local pub back in Wigan! Somehow, the idea of 4 of us seemed safer, I suppose it's the old adage, safety in numbers. It turned into a great afternoon out and carried on well into the night.

Anyway, I digress...

Wigan was a coal and cotton town back in the day, the first coal mine was around 1450, and there were as many as 1000 pit shafts within 5 miles of the town centre, hopefully we won't disappear down one anytime soon.

It was once the territory of a Celtic tribe called the Brigantes. It is believed, the Celtic culture started to evolve around 1200BC and spread throughout Europe. The name Brigantes is reflected in fans who support the Wigan Warriors, the greatest Rugby League team in the world! I often wondered where the name came from.

The Brigantes were subjugated in the Roman conquest following which, the Roman settlement of Coccium established where Wigan stands today.

The popular media would have you believe that Wigan is full of people with grim looks on their faces, women in clogs and shawls, and men smoking Woodbines whilst walking their whippets!
Well, I can tell you, I'm very happy to be here, If I were to do a decisional balance.

Wigan weather is sh**e, but ... I have loads of big coats! Lol!
Tenerife weather is fantastic!
Wigan pies are great, Tenerife has no pie shops!
Wigan Rugby play in Wigan, not Tenerife!
Wigan has Asda, Tesco, Aldi, Lidl, M&S, Tenerife has Mercadona & Lidl! No contest!
In Tenerife, Ale is cheap, but close friends are few and far between
In Wigan, we pay a bit more, but the company's great!
I'd say 4-1 to Wigan!

My hometown was made "famous" by George Orwell in his book "The Road To Wigan Pier", first published in 1937. The first part of this work documents his sociological investigations of the bleak living conditions among the working class in Lancashire and Yorkshire in the industrial north of England before World War II.

After just 2 months in the North, Orwell jumped on the train back south and observed a young woman as he was passing Wigan on the train as quoted below. I don't think the people of Wigan have ever forgiven him for the picture he painted.

The Road to Wigan Pier, George Orwell

"At the back of one of the houses a young woman was kneeling on the stones, poking a stick up the leaden waste pipe which ran from the sink inside and which I suppose was blocked... She looked up as the train passed, and I was almost near enough to catch her eye ... it wore the most desolate, hopeless expression I have ever seen... She knew well enough what was happening to her and understood as well as I did how dreadful a destiny it was to be there in the bitter cold, on the slimy stones of a slum backyard, poking a stick up a foul drainpipe.

The first sound in the mornings was the clumping of the mill-girls' clogs down the cobbled street."

The Leeds Liverpool Canal wends its way through Wigan only 5 minutes from home. Our "neck of the woods" is surrounded by beautiful Lancashire countryside. We are barely 20 miles from the coast, with many lovely places on our doorstep.

I often go for a stroll in nature which is only 5 mins from home, I wonder if George Orwell managed to take in the sights and be mindful of the beautiful local scenery? I doubt it!

Contemporary Wiganers include Richard Ashcroft, lead singer of the Verve, and other band members who studied at a local college. Kay Burley of Sky news fame was born in Wigan. Another three good Wigan lasses... Corrie actresses, Georgia Taylor (Toyah Battersby), Eva Pope (barmaid Tanya Pooley) and Hollyoaks actress Davinia Murphy (Jude Cunningham). The infamous Ian McKelland although born in Burnley was brought up in a house opposite Mesnes Park Wigan, his father being and Engineer for the local authority. There ya go, we're well bred in Wigan. The list goes on and on!

So... be a devil, put Wigan on your Bucket List, remember it's not all Slums and Slag Heaps. When you're coming, drop me a line, we'll enjoy a pint or two of the local brew ... and I'll show you the sights

Chapter 17

Looking After My Elf

It's one of the treasures that money cannot buy! If you're blest with good health you are very rich. It is something that we all tend to take for granted when we have it, and usually only occurs to us once our wellbeing starts to wane for whatever reason.

The question is ...

"What is good health?"

Years ago in 1978, when I was training to be a nurse, health was very much based on a 'medical model' ... the absence of disease or illness. Not so ...

It's what you decide it is, so, for example, you can have several underlying health conditions which are well managed and feel you enjoy good health. If I can do the things I want to do and make memories, enjoying the company of those I love, I consider myself to be healthy. For me, it is very much to do not only with how I feel physically, but also mentally.

I remember an old friend who was getting on in years visiting his GP because he wasn't feeling well, he had not been accustomed to seeking medical help because he had enjoyed particularly good health. When the Dr started to investigate his health issue, it meant he had to have tests which had him backwards and forwards to the hospital, something he hadn't been used to. One day whilst talking to his Dr, he told him,

"I've never bin reet since a turned 87!"

If only we were all so lucky!

When I talk about health, what I really mean is all round health, so physical, mental, spiritual, social. Each has an impact on the others in my experience. In my head, I'm still 21, even sometimes 16 or younger. I can do everything in my head, but although the spirit is willing, sometimes the flesh is weak!

Good health, in my opinion, is also subjective, if I feel mentally on top of the world, I can put up with minor hiccups, my knees don't feel so painful. If I sleep well, my mood is good, I feel refreshed which helps keep me motivated which has the knock-on effect of me feeling happy. It gives me a great perspective on life, and I don't really notice my pain.

The point is that happiness determines how well I feel. During the pandemic, I'm sure I'm not the only one who has been affected by the constant whittering, daily death figures, number of positive cases. Early in the pandemic, I made a considered decision that hanging on every word from Boris and Co was not good for my mental Elf! Don't think I don't understand how serious it is, I simply do what I can do, so follow the rules, HFS and keep busy.

I'm a great believer in there being little point in ruminating about things you can't control. By the way, that doesn't mean I don't worry ever!

I have come to this way of thinking following years of dealing with depression and anxiety and now in my Autumn years, lol, I am at the point where I walk Rover, he doesn't walk me! Don't get me wrong, depression has caused a few potholes in the road, but I can honestly say, it's never really caused a massive derailment. I have also come to accept that's part of me and because I'm less concerned about what people think of me, I'm happy in my own skin. These days good health to me revolves around feeling happy.

In my youth, I used to go roller skating, and I remember only about 3 or 4 years ago, my lovely granddaughter Holly and I were looking for an afternoon out. I got this bright idea and off we went to the roller rink in town, it gave me a real buzz pulling on the skates and took me back in time to those heady days at the Navada Bolton. We had a fabulous afternoon, but not before I had gone ass over tit and landed unceremoniously on the deck. I was just glancing round hoping no one had seen me when the stewards came racing over, how embarrassing, I don't think they were used to having grannies on the rink. In my head, I can also do a handstand, daft owd bugger!

So even when we're getting on in years, we can be fit & well, but one thing I can now admit is, that although I have always had the opportunity to optimise my health, even though I've not always done so. I spent a considerable number of years being a slave to tobacco and am thankful that I have managed to escape that addiction. I started smoking at school, basically everyone smoked in those days, both my parents were smokers, so at home, like most households, we would chat through a haze of smoke. The whole place, although we didn't realise it at the time, would be stained from the smoke Uggh! The change in social conditions to today where most people who smoke go outside is testament to the ills of the habit.

Obviously, I knew full well that it wasn't good for me but lived obliviously in denial like most smokers. I never imagined I could live without what my mother called coffin nails, I really surprised myself. Having said that, even now, in a moment of weakness, especially paired with the demon drink, I can happily puff away on a fag, even convince myself it's ok! Thankfully, I don't often get intoxicated these days, I'm more for just a few quiet glasses of wine accompanied by food, pleasant atmosphere and company. I've become boring in my old age.

Maybe a bit of what you fancy does ya good! "Everything in moderation", my old Nan would say. She

used to have Sanatogen Tonic Wine with 2 raw eggs mixed in with milk every morning ... Ughh! She lived to 89 years, maybe she was pickled. I remember when she took ill shortly before she passed away, the Dr called to see her. She also liked a drop of Whisky and confined to bed in 1989, poorly, she would point to the wardrobe and request her favourite tipple. I was a student nurse at the time and was at the house when to Dr came, my aunty asked him about the whisky. The Dr looked astounded, and advised it wasn't a good idea with her medication. I remember asking him ...

"Are you trying to tell us she won't live to see a hundred if she doesn't stop drinking?"

He smiled when I said she needed a bit of TLC, I knew she was dying, and it seemed to me a little harsh to deny her the one thing she enjoyed. He nodded and wished nan all the best and left. I hope the person looking after me on my deathbed has a sympathetic approach, I'm a terrible patient and certainly will be requesting a drop of Courvoisier!

It's taken me 60+ years to reach the point where I'm now fulfilling the recommended 5 a day, I take vitamins and probiotics and actively try to eat a healthier diet. When I was in my early career, I used to be mad busy. I would often skip meals, go to work without breakfast, mainly because I'd be full up on tea and cigs before I set out, and I'd have a couple of cigs in the car on the way to work. I might grab a pie for dinner and a buttered barm (good Wigan food) however, I have to say, I didn't have any problems with weight back then. As I've got older, the saying *"A moment on the lips, a lifetime on the hips"* is the rule! I've become painfully aware that carrying extra weight is not a good idea with my now arthritic knees taking the toll. The legs that used to be able to cock over a 500cc motorbike even have a problem lifting to negotiate a pair of knickers. Adjustments in my eating have made a difference although it's been a trial during the pandemic! The pounds have been on and off like a bride's nightie.

I've become boring in my old age! I spent most of it racing through my life like being on a fast train journey, not taking opportunity to admire the view.

Basically, I have started to take life a little bit slower in order to admire the beautiful view. I try to savour each moment, that way you do more with your time. When I walk, I take notice of my surroundings and usually punctuate it with pictures which I share on social media, with a promoting good mental health message. Time has somehow become more precious as I'm getting older. Don't misunderstand, I am not sitting on the settee waiting for God, I've too much to do! A friend of ours Colin, always says, "The older you get climbing the tree, the thinner the branches" and he's absolutely right!

I get genuine pleasure from noticing my surroundings when I'm out walking. The other day, the smell of the hedgerow was wonderful, it reminded me of my youth when we used to go down the woods. Just now, all the hedgerows are overgrown, and all the little wildflowers are blossoming. Covid has enabled nature to explode and the colours are just brilliant!

I need daily brain food to nourish my body and soul, I'm a thinker, sometimes too much actually. I'm passionate about raising awareness of mental health issues, and I would never hide the fact that it's part of me. I'm happy in my own skin! In my opinion, everyone should look after their mental health, there are so many demands on everyone, it is easy to feel the effects of stress. It has a knock-on effect on every aspect of your life. There are also great challenges to mental health for young people who are impacted by social media and expected images of how people should have a certain size/ image to be in with the in crowd. I worry about my grandchildren and the possibility of the impact on social media on their self-esteem and confidence. I think it would be a great idea for everyone to have a media fast every so often to free up some thinking space, sometimes I definitely feel my hard drive is full-up or I'm not really syncing with the cloud.

At the beginning of this chapter, talking about overall health, I included 'spiritual' health, then I got to thinking what did I mean? Well, I've had a search through my grey matter and what I really mean is it's to do with the 'ether' or psychological well-being.

My conclusion is, it includes how you feel about yourself, self-esteem, if you're happy with your moral compass, how you feel about your relationships. It's whether you feel happy in your own skin. In my experience, if you don't feel happy, it has a negative impact on your overall existence. I have a lot of respect for His Holiness the Dalai Lama, his focus is the pursuit of happiness.

I would recommend his book 'The Art of Happiness'

Whether a person has a 'faith' or relationship with a higher being or God is, to me, very personal, and is not up for discussion. I personally do have a great relationship with God and find my faith keeps me grounded, apart from the law of the land, I am bound by God's law. It's personal to me and I wouldn't force my views onto any other person.

Chapter 19

Be Kind to your Mind

I couldn't in all honesty write a book about my life without mentioning the impact of depression.

It's not going to be a maudlin tale this because I sort of approach depression with a knowing smile these days. The fact of the matter is that poor mental health is caused by "what you don't see". It's clinical, social, situational, reactive, it's not caused by the person, and they can't simply "pull themselves together".

The thing that most makes me smile is when they say, "It's good to talk", but what people don't say is "but not to me" because people still in this day and age don't get it. Its simply that if you don't experience it, depression is very hard to quantify or understand. It's ok to talk about your heart attack or haemorrhoids, even around the dinner table, but OMG please don't tell me you're depressed. "You mean fed up?" ... "No" For me, depression f**ks up my sense of humour.

At its worst, it's like having a bad day every day, but for me, it's very rarely at it's worst. It makes you feel isolated, even in a room full of people, a person who feels depressed may sometimes be as well on the moon. If you notice a friend or relative who is not their normal self, you might assume they're in a bad mood, or have fallen out with you ... or just maybe they're suffering from depression?

It would be fair to say that things have come a long way, because a few years ago, they would have plugged me in to the electric. Alternatively, I might have ended up in an institution with high walls where no one could see me.

When there's a report about another person committing suicide (even the predictive text didn't want to type that word then lol) people say, "What did he / she have to be depressed about?" The simple answer is nothing, or a myriad of things. Imagine if you had a heart attack and that was the question? What have you done to get a heart attack now? Bloody unreasonable I'd say, especially today of all days ... Bloody inconsiderate these folks who die when they're not supposed to ...

Maybe I'm cynical, but, as a young student nurse, patients used to present themselves or be brought to accident and emergency following an overdose of drugs, an attempted suicide. The treatment back then, was to pump the stomach of the person to remove the tablets, maybe the only way? On reflection, I don't really think they were treated with dignity or respect back in the day. It was like "another bloody overdose, when we're so busy!" I have to say, it wasn't the fault of the staff, they were not trained to look after patients with mental health issues, and even now, the services around supporting people with serious mental health needs are sadly lacking. Talking therapies ... ie "It's good to talk" are scarce at best, services seem to me to be fighting fires, simply putting on plasters to hide the sores.

Ask yourself, have you ever heard anyone say ...

"It's a coward's way out ... suicide"

"They don't think of the people they leave behind, it's selfish".

Just take a minute to think about those remarks, a person who takes their own life does not simply fit into any of those. The truth is that you have to be in an extremely dark place to have the courage to kill yourself. At that moment in time, the person attempting to kill themselves thinks no one cares about them, they genuinely think the world would be a better place if they were not putting such a burden on everyone. Let's face it, no one .... In their right mind, would kill themselves. It alarming how many young men are taking their own lives, I could probably name half a dozen locally over recent months.

What strikes me is, when we're talking about illnesses which affect approx 2:10 people and that's probably an understatement in the current pandemic. On the evening news tonight I listened to a report which told of a young chap from Liverpool who suffered a mental health breakdown in the Northwest, the only bed in a suitable mental health unit was 3 hours travel away, WTF? I'm blest, because I've always had a good support network and been able to access professional help. My GP, has been brilliant, my manager when I was a Health Visitor, a shining example of how a manager should be.

I personally have experienced talking therapies and alternative therapies and have a very good opinion of them. Talking therapies help you to identify if there is a reason for your episode, helps you to identify what YOU can do about it. I found it very empowering and once I realised that some of my depressive episodes were caused by taking on too much, always being the hostess with the mostest! over the years I've learned to look after myself ... my mental Elf!

There is no quick fix, no pills to sort everything out, but they are useful to help you to see the wood for the trees until you feel better. Most anti-depressants help to restore happy hormones/ seratonin, added to which being active and exercise stimulates endorphins which increase mental well-being. I ask myself "What can I do to make myself feel better?" A good walk helps, exercise stimulates the production of happy hormones, swimming, gardening, even getting stuck into housework ... Loads is the answer and that's not just me, I mean you too.

Routine is a good start; self-care is especially important. In this crazy world we live in, there's never time to have 5 minutes to ourselves, (unless we make time).

I have probably spent the greater part of my life actually caring about what people think, but as I'm getting on a bit, I have come to realise that I have no control over what others do, say or think.

It's even more poignant these days when every bugger has an opinion about everyone. Not only do they say things that really affect others, they publish their vile abuse on social media for all the world to see. I really think SM platforms have a lot to answer for, back in the day, social media was someone telling you that something had been said. Most times you didn't notice it, there's a lot to be said for 'out of sight out of mind'.

I can't influence what folks write, but I can 'snooze' or unfollow toxic people off my part of the www because they are how/ who they are, and I can take it or leave it. It's far better to accept that's something I have no control over than ruminate in it for hours/days and cause myself stress.

I think it also helps to be mindful of the rules of the politically correct brigade who, in my opinion are barking mad. Personally, I don't mind what anyone does with their own life, we're all human beings. To me, you can love whoever you want to love, function in whatever way suits you, as long as you're not harming someone else, breaking the law.

Don't tell me that the terms mother & father have to be dumped in favour of biological person who carried the baby/ birthing partner, across the board. No problem if you want to adopt different terms, but don't try to impose them on me! The 21st century world's already past mad … rant over.

I now don't use my precious energy getting involved in other people's drama, rather be in the audience these days. I still stress about stuff, but I soon catch myself and put a stop to it. I have a friend in whom I was confiding once, I was stressing about a person who's behaviour, in all honesty wasn't worth my breath. I was telling my friend about her, and in the event, gave me the best piece of advice ever …

"Delete her from your phone book, email, social media, erase her from your mind, treat the whole thing like she doesn't exist!" She was absolutely right, because since I "rubbed her out" she no longer causes me stress, in fact I feel sorry for her. It is really helpful for me to realise that I don't have to put up with toxic people.

I always used to think I could "fix" everything for everyone. It took up a lot of my energy and caused me stress because, I would invest a lot of time & effort, trying to prevent a friend or relative going down what I thought was the wrong path, then the person concerned would do something entirely different. My daughter hit the nail on the head when she advised me "You don't have to set yourself on fire mum to keep everyone else warm"

I'll never be a person who doesn't care about others around me, or who doesn't offer help to a person in need, but in many cases, I've invested in people who don't really invest in me in return, in some cases, when I feel vulnerable or need help, I look around and my perception is that there's no one there. Not that I help people for reward, I don't really care to get anything back, but sometimes, it's nice if folks recognise the effort, you have put in.

I've learned to let go of relationships which are one sided. I acknowledge that people must make their own decisions and mistakes in life. I can't protect everyone from the consequences of their actions, no matter how painful I might find it, especially when the person is close to my heart. I'm always there if someone has a fall, most people who know me, are aware of that. By backing off and relieving myself from the worry, I now feel more content.

Throughout my life, there is no one who has been more critical of me than myself, I set myself such high standards/ goals that historically I haven't left myself much room for error. I now realise that no one notices except me. That's been another source of stress which has contributed to my history of depression and anxiety. It's a pity it's taken me 62 years to realise it. I don't think it's traditionally British to like ourselves, but once I started to become my own best friend, things stopped bothering me so much.

Chapter 20

Routines & Rituals in

The Big Mother House

I'm wondering, and reflecting on what is the formula for making me tick? I'm a great believer in routine in life, that doesn't mean I don't do anything spontaneous, of course I love to just take off at a minute's notice. I mean the ordinary things of life and how they are punctuating the day. There is, for me a difference between routine and ritual. Routine is the "mundane" tasks I do on auto pilot, in the same order each day. They are things that are necessary to keep the merry go round going but also include things we don't notice we do like having a brew that we do automatically. Ritual comes with more 'intention', over time, I've built intention into the routine which makes it more a purposeful, enjoyable, meaningful and part of life. So, if I can explain what I mean with some examples ...

My 'Ritual' brew is not just 'needed to keep me hydrated" I treat it like an important, mindful minute. Tea tastes nicer from a nice cup! , a certain favourite T bag, a certain strength, with the right amount of sugar and milk. Sometimes topped off with a tasty little biscuit.

Brandy tastes nicer from a crystal brandy glass, preferably middle sized, with one piece of ice. There have been occasions where the moment has been completely spoiled because there was no intention for it to be that way.

One evening in the local, a place where the same people frequented on the same day of the week, at the same time, if you get what I'm saying. I was one of two people whose tipple was Brandy. We walked in, the other brandy drinker was sat in her usual spot at the bar. My OH ordered and the bar lady delivered my double brandy into a half pint glass asked if she should add ice and placed it onto the bar. My OH immediately said to her...

"Have you no brandy glasses love?"

She looked at the brandy glass in front of the other lady sat at the bar and told him although they normally have two brandy glasses, she couldn't locate the other one. She then had a lightbulb moment as she spotted it. She lifted it down from the shelf where it was being used for small change tips, tipped out the change and then proceeded to start to pour my brandy into it, completely ruined the intention!

She obviously had no idea of the ritual that made it special!

Routine was, to me, a little out of my control when I was a wage slave! Get up, share a brew, kids to school, office, workday, home, get the tea on, after tea hour, TV then bed.... in the words of the song

You load sixteen tons and what do you get?
another day older and deeper in debt,

St Peter, don't you call me, 'cause I can't go,
I owe my soul to the company store...

Looking back, even then, I arranged my diary so that I didn't skip lunch every day, because that was an agreement with myself to look after my mental Elf in the early days of developing self care. I had realised that my depression episodes could creep up on me if I took my eye completely off the ball.

When I was a Health Visitor, I would see colleagues frantically trying to keep up with paperwork in the mad hour 4-5pm, answering phone calls, between fulfilling the need to complete record within 24 hours in order for records to stand up in court if ever the need presented itself.

I made an executive decision to add intention and make it a more positive part of my day by taking my notes with me to my visits, spending 5 minutes at the end of each visit to complete them. I then read through them with the mum or parent, which I believed increased the trust and transparency between us. The only exceptional circumstances where I would veer off course, leaving records to write in the office was in cases of safeguarding children, and then I wrote rough notes in the visit. My contact hour between 4-5 became less of a chore, I worried less about my notes and was able to think straight when answering calls.

Increasing the intention adding ritual, really improved my day!

I recognise that when I was younger, and running the household, life was very different, as enjoyable, but different. One of the highlights of my week was Wednesday days off 'routine', similar to 'Off Piste" which was very enjoyable but different. I was blest with the company of my grandson Joe, just magic! We developed the wonderful bond and relationship which we still have now he is an adult.

I remember one particular Wednesday afternoon, we were baking. I can see him in my mind's eye stood on a little stool in the kitchen, bowl on the worktop mixing cake batter. I would talk him through the process and sometimes go off on a tangent chatting about stuff which came into his little head. I feel a happy 'glow' thinking of it. Then the conversation followed...

"Nan, are you married?"

"Well, of course Joe"

"Really, who you married to?"

"Who do you think I'm married to?... Grandad of course, silly"

"My Grandad John?"

He smiled then I could see the cogs turning in his little head, I told him that after we had finished our baking, we could sit together and look at the pictures of our wedding. You may have already read earlier that my OH and I met when he already had our 2 eldest offspring, so when he saw the pictures, he was pointing our all the people he knew at the wedding, like his mum & dad. Then came the burning question...

"Nan, where was I when you got married?"

"Well, let me tell you" I paused and saw the expectant look on his face and said, "You were in Heaven Joe, waiting for your head."

It was something my OH's mum used to say. He jumped off the settee as if he had experienced a lightbulb moment and discovered a link to where he thought Heaven was. He put his hands on his hips and then came the retort...

"Nan, was I there with all the dead people?" Before I had time to think on the answer, we both laughed as he changed the subject,

"Will the cakes be done now? His belly still takes priority over philosophy even these days!

Life these days, for many, is just what I'd call 'Bedlam', employers expecting 200%, working all hours, and the current climate of the 'C' word pandemic has meant that home has also now become work for many. It takes a lot of adjusting to be disciplined enough to be able to treat your home as your workplace. It starts by having a dedicated 'office space' where you associate doing work, not you living room sofa, in front of the TV, because then your sofa becomes your workplace, so how do you then relax with the family in your leisure time, if you're 'in the office' , if you get my drift.

To me, ordinary stuff is wonderful, it's what keeps me grounded, it's my safety net, and probably yours although if you've never thought about it, you may not realise. If I'm in a routine, most things feel good in my world. I'm going to bore you now and tell you what I do in a day.... and then I want you to write down what routines and rituals you have too... you'll be surprised.

Creature of habit, I'm a Tetley's Drinker, whether early or late, doesn't make a difference, I can't really function until I've had a brew. It a sort of waken up routine. I buy them in a bag of 600! Years ago, returning to work after having our daughter Claire, my OH would carry her through to our room then we would share a half hour listening to the radio and having a brew, our older two were at High school by the time she was starting school so they were self-managing, so this was before leaving to deliver her and the other kids to school and making my way to the office.

She still likes to have a hug beside me, especially if she's had a few sherbets. She has a great sense of humour. When we've had a drink, if she's staying over, I'm usually the first to retire, usually, 10-15 mins later, I get a little tap on the door... "it's only me". She pulls back the duvet and climbs in usually fully clothed and snuggles in next to me. A conversation ensues, she shushes me a few times then flakes out... it's wonderful!

Back to the here and now after that short diversion.

Enjoying my brew, I watch BBC news on my iPad, never ITV because up to a few weeks ago, they had the most argumentative, arrogant presenter I had ever had the displeasure of listening to. He was simply noise pollution personified, he walked out after a disagreement with another presenter about the prince and the actress! Bliss...

I don't dwell too much on the news, this is about the only time of day I would give it my airtime. I think there's far too much fake reporting goes on and, half the time I think they're making it up! And those words 'Fake News' are probably the most sensible words that came out of Trump's mouth.

Sometimes I'm awake at 6 am when my OH sets out for his morning walk. He puts his feet out of bed and gets dressed (showering later) and once he's got his kit on, he goes to the window to check the score on the 'puddle o meter'. If it's favourable, he turns out for his stroll. Not before he's given me a bit of encouragement ...

"Come on, let's go."

Once I've ascertained that he's not actually addressing me, and is talking to his invisible friend, I usually turn over till he's gone! Morning walks are definitely not my bag!

If I rise very early with the birds and OH, I absolutely savour every moment till I rise between 8.30-9am. I usually spend some time writing, depending on the hour, just now, as I write it's almost 8am, but I started at 6.30.

I can see you rolling your eyes, but I'm on a journey to enlightenment and I need my peace and a girl needs to rest to keep young & beautiful.

I don't usually go downstairs in pyjamas, I shower at 8.30-9am and follow my morning ritual, no soap on my face, cleanse, moisturise, check my wrinkles, sometimes I think I'd be better investing in some Polyfilla. My girls are both Botox fans, I don't really get it, they're both so young and beautiful, it makes me roll my eyes. I think I'm past my sell by date but there's plenty of time on my "use by", even if my eggs *are* scrambled.

Then I put a bit of tutti on to and do my hair. Once I've completed my ritual, I then get dressed as if I were going on a nice day out, maybe, especially during lockdown as mum would have said "you're all dressed up and nowhere to go."

In my mind, my ritual sets me up for the day, it puts me in the mood and motivates me, it makes me feel alive!

Sometimes I get a enquiring look from my sweetheart, and the question "You off out? he doesn't realise it is my ritual to keep me happy! I have learned what contributes to my feel-good factor, and image.

He has rituals too, he doesn't necessarily realise that's what it is, but I notice them.

"A place for everything, and everything in its place"

"A tidy site is a nice site" from his building days.

"Never pay anyone to do anything you can do yourself."

Once up, breakfast ritual, all nicely prepared, usually by my sweetheart (he is breakfast chef), not rushed, quiet. I have a mental list of my To Do's which I consider whilst having my quiet breakfast time. I always clean the kitchen am, it gives me a good feeling when completed. My added enjoyment (ritual) is the traditional Irish music playing, joining in, having a jig. It's done in no time!

So, my day progresses...

Once I have all my jobs done, it signals time for a more leisurely pursuits, TV, catch up on inane little programmes like Bake Off and The Sewing Bee, gardening, painting.... The list is endless. At some point, I will have a surf, think about my blog post for the day, usually during a brew.

Like most people I have ritual social media things to do, #Hashtags, Instagram posts, Facebook & Twitter feeds.

There's one thing I can guarantee, there's never a dull moment in the Big Mother House.

Try having a think about What rituals you have; it will surprise you ...

Be like the robin ..
Sing like no-one is
Listening 😊

Chapter 21

In Pursuit of Happiness

In the car on the way home from Asda, singing along to the radio considering the rest of my day, a jingle came on. It was advertising the latest competition, for just a £2 stake by text, an entry to win a Volkswagen Golf, a holiday in Tenerife and £50,000 Wow! How fabulous that would be, it raised my mood just thinking of it.

Most of us, mere mortals will never be fortunate enough to experience the absolute joy of that moment when the presenter rings a random mobile and it turns out to be our number.   If that is not to be the case, what makes us happy!

I'm a great believer that everyone is in persuit of happiness in this crazy world we live in, it doesn't happen without effort, it's something that has to be worked on and nurtured.

According to Dictionary.com the definition of happiness is simply:

-noun

1 the quality or state of being happy.

2 good fortunes; pleasure; contentment; joy

Bit vague I'd say, and everyone's idea of it will be different.

For me, at this time of my life, happiness is peace of mind, no dramas, no circuses, no monkeys, Oh and ...

- ✓ 8 hours uninterrupted sleep per night, well including loo breaks...
- ✓ The ability to do a hand stand even if only in my dreams.
- ✓ Absence of arthritics ...
- ✓ Less wrinkles, or more effective poly-filler!
- ✓ For the folks who do "pure cremations" to delete me from their mailing list!
- ✓ Brandy that doesn't get me drunk (because I'm going off hangovers)

My post today comprised of one brochure for River cruises from saga, a copy of gardener's world, and an invitation to join the pure cremations funeral plan and stuff asking if you've made a will. You know that you are well up the branches of the tree when people start suggesting you get a funeral plan. I already recognise envelopes that are from Over 50's plans so I can put them straight in the recycling bin. It's just a good job I've got a sense of humour. I heard an Irishman talking about old age, it made me laugh ...

"What's the difference between a house and a home?"
"A home is where they put you when they get you out of the house!"
"My daughter asked for a loan secured on the will, which she then said was a short term loan!"

I remember when I was younger before I flew the nest away from my ma and pa, my mum had a very different view of happiness, she would cook certain things, let dad have control of the telly, do anything for a quiet life to keep him happy, which in turn, kept her happy! I love the new normal myself, "Happy wife ... Happy Life", how things have changed... for the better.   I noticed a birthday card this afternoon, scene, Bingo Hall, the caller announces the next number is two voluptuous, curvy, beautiful, empowered ladies ... 88 Ha! Very funny, girls of my generation were used to the old politically incorrect terminology, we didn't take it quite so literally, in any case great to see it's been given its comeuppance!

So back to happiness ...
These days, there is so much demand made on people to keep up with the Kardashians, social media, botox, face lifts, tucks and braces in an effort to be beautiful. They're all beautiful already in my humble opinion, it's a wonder anyone is happy with their lot.

For me, it's being content with life ... as it is. Although generally, folks would like more money to ease the burdens of life, there only so many material possessions you can own. I personally don't need a lot to keep me happy, just enough to be able to have a pie, a crust and a pint or two, well Brandy actually, a double ... with ice!

When I look around at my 'things' there are very few I couldn't do without. God forbid, if there was a reason why I lost them, most, with the exception of one or two of my prized possessions which are primarily things with sentimental value to me, things that were passed on from my most loved, or gifted to me by my nearest and dearest. Grandma's eternity ring, mum´s beads and bracelet, and some of mum´s belongings, plus jewellery that I wear on a daily basis which is all sentimental. Oh, and Grandad's boxing picture and Grandad Harold's war medal. I have my precious items, which are probably not worth a lot in monetary terms together in an imaginary 'time capsule' box in my mind. I've actually had another look around and it would probably stretch to a suitcase if I'm honest.

I've heard the saying "money can't buy happiness", but being rich and miserable is better that being happily skint", many a true word spoken in jest I suppose, however, there has to be more to life than money. Essentially, I'm blest in every which way, I recognise that we're not all in the same boat, in fact some are on a luxury cruise liner and others are barely rowing, but just because someone appears materially deprived doesn't always mean they're not happy.

I think it's about beliefs and approaches and expectations of life.   There's a lot to be said about acceptance that nothing is permanent. Situations change on a daily basis and adapting to and accepting change, for me, has a lot to contribute to overall happiness. When I was a kid, although both mum and dad worked to keep the house going, they didn't have a great deal of disposable income.   Despite not being able to have "everything and a bag to put it in" as mum would have said, it was a happy home. Mum and dad had a bit of a turbulent relationship at times, rows were common, silent meals at least every third week (night turn). Looking back, we accepted it as normal and although it was not great seeing adults arguing, we learned to deal with it.

As kids, in the summer we would set out with our friends and go playing on a rope swing in the woods equipped with a pop bottle full of water and a packed lunch of jam butties which we would share between us. When I was at grammar school, one of the holidays was to Norway, but my parent couldn't afford the cost, so I couldn't go. I have harboured a desire to see the fjords up to the present day and finally have booked a bucket list cruise to Norway. It's only taken 50 years to get round to it for me, and a bit of persuasion to convince my OH we should go somewhere on holiday that might require boots and a big jacket.

(Ps it's now been rearranged 3 times due to the 'C' word, but adaptation is a wonderful quality, at least we've something to look forward to)

Happiness can sometimes be confused with pleasure or joy. Individual events or good fortune, getting a new job, a pay rise, undoubtedly contributes to happiness at the time, but to achieve overall happiness? My view is that happiness is the baseline, then when extra good things happen, adding into the cake mix a bit of joy, we experience an happy hormone rush and great enjoyment, then after a little while it subsides and we go back to the normal baseline, ticking along.

It's taken some thinking about to identify what exactly makes me happy. It's mainly to do with meaningful stuff, it's really hard to define, but when I do or achieve things that mean something to me, it makes me happy. I have to say, now I'm trying to explain it, it's very complex. It's not simply temporary joy like winning something (usually a tenner on postcode lottery lol) which makes me smile and gives me the hope I might win the £30,000! My response to what I would do if I won the lottery would be, "Make a lot of people very happy". There's not a lot of things I need which would greatly enhance my quality of life, now, money could buy me an operation probably quicker than waiting on a list, but it couldn't guarantee that my operation would be successful. One of the very things that money definitely can't buy is health. If you're young now, my best advice to you would be to take your opportunities whilst you're well enough, because once you start getting niggly health issues, it impacts on everything you do.

There used to be a little character drawing with captions 'Love is', well in a similar vein, I'm going to try to give some examples...

Happiness is ...

- ✓ Giving a little surprise to someone, it makes me happy to see them smile, or imagine how it will improve their day if they receive a little something in the post... It was one of the joys in my younger days, when I had pen friends, in those days there was very little junk mail and the slap of the post on the mat signalling a letter from afar was magic.

- ✓ Telephoning someone out of the blue, or a coffee with an old friend, which is priceless.

- ✓ Giving a stranger a bunch of flowers.

- ✓ Paying a coffee forward for the person next in the queue.

- ✓ Giving, to me, is as rewarding as receiving, if not more so. The most precious gifts you can give or receive are your time, friendship, a listening ear, and love for a fellow being. Ironically, all immeasurable and cannot be bought no matter how much money a person has.

✓ 5 minutes peace away from the noise pollution

✓ Watching a Blackbird in the garden with his offspring sharing some bread.

✓ Meeting an old friend for coffee

✓ Laughing with my sweetheart about something daft

✓ I personally get a happy buzz when I experience a bit of retail therapy, I can understand why people become addicted to shopping, especially during the lockdown. I have come to realise; I can get the buzz even if I buy myself a very small treat like a nail varnish or lipstick and it's not quite so expensive as shopaholic ... ing can be! The funny thing is, I also get a buzz if I take something back and get a refund, Lol Winner Winner ...

Keeping out of drama, which years ago would have had me running round trying to fix everything for everyone. I think it's because I've come to accept that there are some things even, I can't fix Lol ...that, in itself reduces my stress and increases my happiness. I no longer feel I need to be all things to all men ... and women. Someone very close to me gave me a bit of friendly 'advice'.

"You don't have to set yourself on fire, to keep everyone else warm".
So ... "What would make you happy?"
Is it to do with?
Relationships?
Money? If you won the lottery, would all your troubles be over, would you be happy?

Kids?

Work?

No worries?

John was recently talking to our seventeen-year-old grandson Joe, who was as usual complaining about his lot, too much work, college, chores, his quota of sleep. The general theme was how to get everything without having to put the effort in, like I wanna be fit, but I can't be doing with the exercise shi*e. The question on the table was ...

"If I gave you £10,000, would it make you happy?"

He quickly responded in the negative, but added,

"If you want to give it to me, I'll happily take it."

I'm a little easier to please, there are undoubtedly some good things about being old enough to need a knee replacement. I get free prescriptions, free eye tests and believe it or not, double points on my Boots Advantage card! All these things contribute to my overall happiness.

Oh ... and this morning I got an email, 'good news from Lotto, log into your account'. OMG I've won EuroMillions, a moment of anticipation, then after the message on log in saying we don't have an account with those details, Ta Dah... great news, you've won £2.80 on EuroMillions! We've added it to your account 😄

Anyway, enough of my rambling on, main thing ... don't worry, be happy ...

Chapter 22

Reflecting on Death & People Who have

Toddled off This Mortal Coil

I suppose, I'm pretty philosophical about death and dying. It's part of life because let's face it, none of us are getting out of here alive! I'm open to discussion and respect anyone's opinions of whether there is life after death, reincarnation, or end of the line.... I think I've probably said already that I'm at an age where I get junk mail from the folks at "Pure Cremations" I've made the decision already to be cremated because in my belief, my soul will leave my mortal body which will no longer be needed.

I envision a picture in my mind of a smoking shelter outside the pearly gates overflowing with my nearest and dearest. As the automatic gates swing open there is a beautiful vision of "The Just Inn", a typical looking chocolate box country pub.

When you are newly passed over, St Peter gets all your folks together for a forward welcoming party, all inclusive (of course), pork pies and roasties on the bar and 24 hour service. You see the place is packed out and you're surprised at the reception you're getting, it's only then, you realise how much folks thought of you, and how your life impacted on hundreds of people. Like George in It's a Wonderful Life, I wish I'd known earlier!

Grief and loss only really started affecting me when I was 18 years old. The reason that I rewind to 18 is that although I had experienced the loss of two grandads in the  early 70s, I don't really remember feeling very bereaved. The only way I can explain it is that in my child's eye, I had a different view. When I was 11, just started Grammar school, following the summer holidays, we gathered at The Hollies in "La Salle" on the first morning back. Looking back, I remembered a most beautiful girl in my class called Angela Cleary, she had Auburn red hair down to her waist. As Sr Marie led assembly, we were told that Angela had died in the holidays from an Asthma attack. The sisters offered excellent spiritual support to us in school, it is not until I have started to reflect that I realise, her death was accepted as part of life at that time.

I do remember the funerals of both my grandads but no long-lasting sadness. Life seemed just to go on, I can't really explain why. I feel sadness now 40+ years later, because on reflection, I wish I had known them both into my adult life when I felt greater conscious regard for them. I would have loved to really know them.

I think, when you're a kid, you think everyone is always going to be there. My feeling is that as a child if you have adults around you who behave in a sort of normal manner when there is a bereavement, the child looks to the adult for reassurance and if everything seems okay then it passes ok for the child. Depending on the age of the child, At around seven or eight, when someone dies, the idea that someone has gone permanently is starting to develop. If that person is not immediate to them, it has less of an impact. The older the child/ young person gets, the more impact it has.

I have a memory full of wonderful people who have died, all very special and loved dearly. I have, however, imprinted in my brain, certain memories of people whose death, for whatever reason had a big impact on me. They are mainly people who I never got to say adios to, until we meet again.

So by the time I was 18, I was responding in an adult way. The difference is that back then, I hadn't really developed the faith I have now, although I believed in God, it wasn't such a strong feeling. It is only now that I refer to this beautiful poem by Henry Scott Holland ...

It simply suggests that people who have died step into the next 'room, an interval away', a beautiful concept I think. The poem reminds us that we should never be afraid to talk about our deceased loved ones, and you will have already noticed, I refer to things that people said ... all the time, particularly my mum Lol. They're all chatting in the smoking shelter outside the pearly gates!

Death is nothing at all.
It does not count.
I have only slipped away into the next room.
Nothing has happened.

Everything remains exactly as it was.
I am I, and you are you,
and the old life that we lived so fondly together is untouched, unchanged.
Whatever we were to each other, that we are still.

Call me by the old familiar name.
Speak of me in the easy way which you always used.
Put no difference into your tone.
Wear no forced air of solemnity or sorrow.

Laugh as we always laughed at the little jokes that we enjoyed together.
Play, smile, think of me, pray for me.
Let my name be ever the household word that it always was.
Let it be spoken without an effort, without the ghost of a shadow upon it.
Life means all that it ever meant.
It is the same as it ever was.
There is absolute and unbroken continuity.
What is this death but a negligible accident?

Why should I be out of mind because I am out of sight?
I am but waiting for you, for an interval,
somewhere very near,
just round the corner.

All is well.
Nothing is hurt; nothing is lost.
One brief moment and all will be as it was before.
How we shall laugh at the trouble of parting when we meet again!

Henry Scott Holland

I remember as though it was yesterday the day my grandma Kenyon died, it was a Sunday evening about 7.15pm, mum was working as a barmaid in the local and dad was on afternoon shift at Heinz. I heard a knock on the door, it was a beautiful summers evening, the sky was blue, and the sun was out. It was balmy, if you get my drift. When I open the door, I saw my cousin Margaret stood there, she had a sort of pensive look on her face. Before I could invite her in, she simply said: "Nans died".

We didn't have a phone at the time, so someone had called her, appointing her messenger. What a terrible job to give to someone, I immediately thought that she meant my Nan who was also her Nan. Then she said to me to qualify her message, it's Nanny Kenyon. Well, that wasn't nanny that was grandma!

I stood there frozen to the spot almost in suspended animation, the buses and cars were still going past our house, how could that be when Grandma had died?

Surely not, the day before on Saturday, in the morning, she had come to our house as she always did. She looked perfectly well and I was kicking myself, well I do even now, that on that morning, her last visit, I had left to go to a meeting in Preston barely 10 minutes after she arrived. You know that feeling of... if I had known then what I know now, I would've spent every waking hour making the most of my time with her.

She was 58 years old, one of the loveliest kindest people I've ever met, she was my mentor, one of my best friends in the world. I had an amazing bond with her, I loved my Nan but my bond with Grandma Kenyon was beyond belief!

I think about her most days, but I feel now that she is very close to me spiritually, as I think of all those I have loved who have passed away.

The day that grandma died, my grandad's heart died too. I could cry simply thinking about it, we were all devastated, but for him, it tore out all his heart and soul. After that day he simply didn't want to live anymore, she was the trailer to his tractor, and life didn't ever feel the same for him. He wasn't in very good health, and she had been his lifeline, his sweetheart. I think you will already realise that he was one of my other best mates.
He used to say to me ...

"I wish God would take me".
I used to get really annoyed with him, and say...
"God is probably sat up there disgusted with you... There are plenty of folk in the cemetery who would swap places with you."
He would nod and smile. I wanted him to have the will to carry on, I loved him so dearly, it was so difficult having lost her, I selfishly wanted him to stay around. I used to visit him every day, do his shopping, cook for him, and generally spend time with him. We had great chats about his life, he had a brilliant sense of humour! I think I mentioned in an earlier chapter that he offered to be the guinea pig if I wanted to practice giving injections when I started nurse training. He was gorgeous! If he was here now, I'd hug him so tight and never let go. I felt the loss of him a long time before he died, in fact, I used to pray that God would grant his wish, because he was suffering so much. He didn't have enough breath to walk 50 yards. He passed away in December 1978 aged 63, on the ward where I would eventually end up as Ward Sister.

Over the past 40 years I lost two cousins, taken well before their time. My cousin Lorraine was 6 years my junior and 22 years old when she passed away in 1985. She was a beautiful soul, with long dark brown hair down her back. We didn't see her very often once we were adults, she lived over in Rochdale. As we'd got older and had settled into marriages and long standing relationships, we sort of drifted apart. We always kept in touch by phone occasionally but not often. It's the old thing, you don't ever imagine someone is going to die so young, especially when she's your cousin. Those tragedies happen to other people, don't they?

It was a Friday night and I had taken my mum to the Bingo in Wigan town centre. There were no mobiles back then, so it was difficult to get hold of people. Just as we were focussed on hoping that our numbers would come out, the place was packed, then right out of the blue the caller stopped calling the numbers. The manager climbed up onto the stage and announced, "Is Doreen Maloney in the club?" We both looked at each other, stunned, we were accompanied to the foyer where my mum's brother Ricky was waiting with the news that Lorraine had died. It was incredulous, whatever must have happened, so tragic that the beautiful Lorraine had died? I have to say that even to this day, I can't recall the events leading to her death. I have very fond memories of her, I can see her in my mind's eye, she was the prettiest child you could imagine.

My other cousin was Andrew, he died tragically in a parachuting accident aged just 30. My mum and dad had recently celebrated their 40th wedding anniversary and were on holiday in Turkey. Andrew had paid for his brother to experience a parachute jump as a gift for his 21st birthday and had been persuaded to 'jump' with him. I got the shock of my life when I received the phone call from his distraught mum. He had "accidentally" pulled the emergency release cord and lost his chute at 200ft. Despite deploying his emergency parachute, he died instantly on impact. I still carry feelings of grief from his death and probably will forever.

We had already lost his dad a few years earlier aged 47, my mums younger brother Ricky. He was a hoot; he was full of fun and the heart and soul of any party. I still feel annoyed with him for passing away so suddenly without saying goodbye! He had visited us the day before on Easter Tuesday when Claire was 5 months old. I still remember the conversation; he was making cracks about how bonny she was.
"Bloody hell Denise, what have you been feeding her on?
"Breastmilk, you dumb ass"
"I think I'd have grown on breastmilk too!"
"Well don't let it be another 5 months till you see her again Rick".
We hugged and he left to go to the rugby match...
The next day, while waiting for my Aunty to finish work late afternoon in the local, he died suddenly from a blood clot in his lung. Heartbroken couldn't even describe how I felt.

One of the important factors for me is that over the years, I have fostered a feeling of acceptance of change in my life, nothing is permanent, even life is mostly a series of unplanned events. We have goals, but they are affected by factors which are sometimes out of our control.

Grief is an extremely difficult emotion, it is universal to everyone, yet personal. There are many stages of grief from denial to acceptance, and how you progress through the stages is personal.

Each person goes through the stages at a different pace, so for example, when my dad died 7 years ago, I had spent a week nursing him round the clock, taking turns staying up overnight. During that time, we had the opportunity to chat, I was able to establish with him how much I loved and regarded him and shared his last few days on earth. It was personal between us. I felt resigned to the fact I'd done everything possible to help and support him and was at peace with his passing.

I also think that when a loved one is suffering, we start to grieve whilst they are still with us. It's like grieving the person they once were. With dad, I felt acceptance fairly quickly. Other people may still be at an earlier stage of grief. My faith plays a very big part of my life and certainly helps get me through.

There is just one person for whom my feelings of loss surpass any other, my dear mum, my best friend, my rock. Anyone who has lost their mum will know and instinctively feel what I mean. I could tell my mother anything, especially a risqué joke, we would howl laughing, I'd have her in stitches when helping her in the shower as she marched into old age. There was no embarrassment between us, as she got undressed, I'd start singing "Who let the dogs out" as she lost her bra. I can see her now stood there, legs crossed laughing her head off and telling me I was crackers! I could confide anything in her and she in me. I was indeed blest when God gave out mothers, and fathers too for that matter.

They say you can choose your friends but not your relatives, well on reflection I can't think of anyone I wouldn't have chosen, I have loved them all in their own unique way and still love the ones left behind, even the awkward buggers!

As I'm climbing the tree of life, I also realise that I'm getting closer to the front of God's queue. It's sometimes difficult coming to terms with how getting older impacts, however, I've finally written the dreaded will, I just need to decide on the hymns. If I'm lucky enough to live well into old age, I might see HS2 built... but I doubt it, (I mean HS2) As none of us know, we would all benefit from living life to the full and taking our opportunities. We should cherish the connections we have and make the most of fostering and nurturing close relationships with those we ♡ love.

When I fall off my perch, I would like to think I'd be known as having lived a good long life and have smiled on many of my fellow humans as I passed along

Chapter 2

Trying to make sense of

Spirituality & Religion

When I was reflecting on looking after my Elf in an earlier chapter, I somehow felt I'd left out the 'Spiritual' bit. Generally, my thoughts are that these days it's fashionable to be spiritual, but not religious. I know it's a difficult concept, it's taken me ages to work it out in my head, and I'm going to try to explain what I mean.

According to the Cambridge dictionary:

Religion
Noun:
The belief in and worship of a god or gods, or any such system of belief and worship

Spirituality
Noun:
The quality that involves deep feelings and beliefs of a religious nature, rather than the physical parts of life

Spirituality and spiritual health, I think includes a purposeful life. It includes experience beyond the 'normal'/physical level. I've heard people say, yes, I believe there must be some entity / thing higher than us but I'm not religious. That's fine by me, because I think by saying I'm not religious, they mean they don't go to church. Well, you don't have to, that's up to the individual isn't it ...

So, you can, for example have a connection with nature / Mother Earth / being grounded. To me it includes your ethics, what you think is right and morals or what rules you set your life by. I'm going to try to give you an idea of the sorts of stuff I mean.

If you think of Spirituality in that way, then it doesn't become embroiled in religion, which to me is an entirely different entity. To me, religion is like belonging to a group of like-minded people who have something in common. Religion IS NOT the church, priest, Bishops etc... it is the congregation. I wouldn't particularly ask anyone about their views on religion, hence the saying, don't discuss religion or politics... Sometimes folks take it upon themselves to let you know their views when on

YOUR choice to follow a certain faith. I don't know why, but it's as if you're going to somehow judge them if they're not a part taker in what they see as mumbo jumbo. Personally, I don't mind what anyone believes in their own space ...

"There but for the grace of God, go I."

I don't think it's particularly only self-confessed God botherers use that saying. I personally do believe that God/ Higher being, looks after me and I make no apologies for, my beliefs, it's no detriment to any other person who doesn't agree. I have been reflecting on, what exactly is grace? Maybe the sense of God's unmerited love and favour? I suppose that spiritually, the saying means to me understanding another person's situation and acknowledging that the same could have happened to you, but for the protection of God, or some reason you can't explain. It feels unquantifiable trying to get my head round it, but although it's hard to explain, after thinking of examples, other sayings with the words grace or gracious come to mind, it's here I digress. Forgive me ... Lol.

"Being gracious in defeat".

In our household, Rugby League is our other *religion.* I liken this to when Wigan play Saint Helens, all the Saints speccies take great joy in taunting the Wiganers if we lose. It's exceedingly difficult to take, to be able to say the better team won (as if) but if you're gracious about it (take the flack), without rising to it, then when the tables turn, you can have your day ... Lol, then they can *be gracious in defeat*, somehow, I don't think so, ha!

221

"Fallen From Grace."

My thoughts are that if you fall from grace, you fall out of favour, maybe you are no longer "flavour of the month". Maybe done something to tarnish your reputation? Out of favour with the boss, or anyone for that matter.

I'm trying to recall a time when I *"fell from grace"*. When I was a ward sister, we had a terribly overbearing Nursing Officer and, fortunately for some reason, I was one of her protégés. I was very outspoken even back then, but less than now ... Lol ... in those days Ward Sisters were very respected and great pride was taken in the uniform. One day, she arrived on the ward with this fancy nurses' hat, it was all lace with a big frill from one side to the other sticking up. When I saw it, I wondered how it was going to sit without ruining my hair. My face must have said it all, she instructed me to go and fix it on my bonce, then remarked "you don't like it do you?"
I responded, "It's ok, we'll be able to hang balls off it at Christmas!"
That was the start of me *falling from grace,* it was all downhill from there.

Anyway, back to my thread ... For me, it's like any other relationship you or I choose to engage in. It's personal, it's to do with the human soul, mind or spirit, the psyche. It's an agreement with myself about how I live my life and how I treat the planet and fellow humans. It's just that underpinning my set of rules and high on my list of priorities, is my relationship with a higher being ... God. I don't do or say anything that is prescribed to me, I am my own person, and I won't take exception if you disagree. I don't make any apologies for it, it's part of me, who I am. I'll never refer to it in conversation unless brought up, but I'll never deny it either.

I was once listening to the homily given by a young priest, who was also the hospital chaplain. He described a visit he made to an elderly lady on the ward. He sat down with her and was having a chat. She asked him "Are you Jesus?", he smiled as he told her that he was the chaplain and had come to be a bit of company for her. What I remember from his homily was, he said "When you're a Christian, people should see a little of God in you". That's what I try to aspire to, I think people who treat others as they wish to be treated can spread happiness in the community. What it doesn't mean is that I think people who don't practice a religion don't do good things or behave in a loving caring way towards their fellow beings. My paternal grandfather wrote in his diary "if I can help somebody as I pass this way, then my living will not be in vain". I think he was right.

I am currently following a course entitled uncovering your authentic self and research for my studies led me to a book by Don Miguel Ruiz Titled The Four Agreements. I find it fits very well with Spirituality/Religion.

The book is extremely engaging, based on ancient Toltec wisdom, emanating from Mexico, the 4 agreements are like a simple code of conduct. I think a lot of people will be able to relate to it in their own lives.
Ruiz states:

"Everything we do in life is based on agreements we have made-agreements with ourselves, with other people, with society, with God. But the most important agreements we make are with ourselves. In these agreements, we tell ourselves who we are, how to behave, what is possible and what is impossible "

The four agreements is not based on a particular 'Religion', It is about how individuals make agreements with themselves to do or not do certain things in their lives. Sometimes agreements with ourselves stifle our growth, particularly if they are destructive, for example things based on fear, Eg. If I don't do this, I will prevent this ... Ruiz suggests that agreements based on love help us to grow, one of his 4 agreements is

"Don't take things personally"

Easier said than done, but with a bit of practice you can do it. I reflect on some situations which have arisen in my life.

In particular, one situation with a person very dear to my heart, whom I love dearly, but he always insisted on commenting, particularly on social media, inappropriately. He has a habit of always referring everything to my belief in God ... *"so does this or that not fit in with your God?"*

When the Catholic Church scandal about priests abusing boys in their care emerged, he made a particular point of bringing the subject up with me as if I were responsible? I feel it said more about him than me to be honest and led to communication between us ceasing.

It is several years since I spoke with him, and sadly he omitted to attend my mum's funeral, I'm not sure if that was the reason but, it's very sad indeed. I still love him, if he takes exception to my beliefs that's his affair, but I don't have to be party to it. People are like magazines; you don't have to subscribe to their issues. In the end, I removed myself from the firing line, unfortunately that means we are not in contact directly. I often enquire about his well-being, but I choose not to be involved with his opinions. I feel this resonates with not *taking things personally,* by accepting that's how it is the anger of the 'personal' attack is removed. I can live with it so all's well.

Religion does not define me, neither should attending church, it's how I choose to live my life.

When I first met my OH and our relationship developed into a long-lasting bond, I had a conversation with my priest about going to communion. That being because divorce is not recognised in our church, so our relationship was considered adulterous by some people. I was party to bringing up our children in the faith and I felt it important to set an example to them as their step-in mum. The priest spoke what he believed the letter of the law was, I believe he did not consider how what he said impacted on me. Basically, my OH is my greatest love, I explained to the priest that my children were coming up to making their 1st communion and I planned to stand beside them at communion, and I recognised that my being a divorcee and being in a new relationship with a man I loved, may not be the "right fit" in the church's "law". More recently the church has modernised, thankfully.

He quite nonchalantly said to me,

"Yes, you can go to communion, all you need to do: is stop having an adulterous relationship with this man"

I was, initially offended by his words, I wanted to say to him, you would rather I abandon 2 children and a man I love? It was a big turning point for me. Once I realised that I shouldn't *take it personally,* I could accept that he

225

was simply quoting a prescriptive rule to which he had no control over. I then approached another priest to explore if this was a uniform reaction within the clergy? I received a completely different reception, and it was then, I decided, that I would live my life under my own jurisdiction, and in effect, sort it out directly with God, when I get there! Those were the priest's words to me, and he was correct, I am not responsible to anyone apart from myself.

"Be impeccable with your word". Ruiz suggests that words are the most important part of how you conduct yourself. If you follow the agreement, then by using words positively and with love, then you will realise that your words can make or break another person. Look up the words of ... "If I could turn back time" the pop song made famous by Cher.
"Words are like weapons, they wound sometimes".

It says it all. By using negative or judgemental words, that's what you will reap. It's not rocket science, and in my experience has shown itself day in day out. Gossiping or spreading rumours is like a virus passing around, and we're all aware of how destructive that is.

What comes to mind is Love Thy Neighbour, these days, I think the word love is bandied about without thought.
If I tell someone I love them, it's considered, sincere and comes with actions, I hope the people I love, don't need me to be saying it every fart's end (as mum would say) ... lol.

"Don't make assumptions"

I can relate to this absolutely, I am guilty of assuming that everyone sees life the way I see it especially if I'm

226

tootling along taking my life for granted, which we all do. Sometimes I assume that my sweetheart will disapprove of something or other without asking him or clarifying. I've sometimes already decided in my head, he'll disapprove of whatever it is. I then feel annoyed that he's going to disapprove, when in actual fact I've not even asked him or clarified the point. I think it comes from when I was younger and my dad's responses to my mum.

An example of this is when I go out shopping, I sometimes feel anxious if I'm out more that the time necessary to do the basics. When mum and I went shopping back in my youth, she would be constantly telling me we had to hurry, because "he'll be going mad, we've been out 2 hours, he won't have had a drink etc...". So, 45 years later, I carry the anxiety of my youth and create my own anxiety thinking my OH will be annoyed in the same way. So, the agreement not to make assumptions undoubtedly improves the way we experience life.

If you think about it, if we negatively assume the worst then we cause ourselves untold grief, it usually fuels negatively imagining the future and having the knock-on effect of supporting depression.

Always do Your Best

If you always do your best, then you will achieve your potential in life. Sometimes we let ourselves down by not being fully in the room. No one can ask for more, even if you're working at reduced capacity, you can do your best within the confines of your ability at the time.

Remember to always strive to fulfil your dreams, don't put too much pressure on yourself and ... enjoy each moment. At the end of the day, none of us is getting out alive, nod nod, wink wink, if you get my drift.

Chapter 24

Reaching the Top of the Tree

Is it that time already? When you've spent so much time making a living that you forgot to make a life Lol ... joking! It's great to report I've enjoyed a blest life ... so far, great family, friends, experiences, holidays, fun and games with much more to come, I hope.

It's right what they say, the years fly by without such as a blink, I remember the Millenium when people were predicting that at midnight the computers wouldn't be able to cope with the change in numbers. Were now 22 years in and it seems like only yesterday. I worried about stuff years ago and lost precious time and enjoyment in the process. If time were to jump forward 22 years, I'll be ... a lot older than I am today Lol

Please don't get the impression that I'm negative about retirement or getting older, there are some benefits ... Free Eye Tests and Free Prescriptions Lol!

It's also a great time to take up Ski ... ing! Or **S**pending the **Ki**ds **I**nheritance if you get my drift.

I have to say, it _is_ kind of scary getting closer to the top of the tree and not a thing to dwell on. Currently, life expectancy for a woman, if you're lucky is 81 years 2 months, a little shorter for a man. I'm not sure exactly when it dawned on me that I'm getting nearer the front of Gods queue, but I certainly am aware of it now.

It's an odd feeling when all your offspring have flown the nest and you are expected to give up work and occupy yourself at the same time. All those years striving to get to the end of your working life and reach the magical age "retirement", when you can do as you please. Just as you are dependent on your retirement income, you realise that the most valuable currency is time ... All those days when I said I was too busy!

In view of my diminishing time left on earth, I have managed to develop the ability to truly take each day, being mindful, enjoying the moment, being present. When you notice each moment and experience, its easy to pack in loads of stuff.
If you keep a diary of your week, you can fit in lots of different activities and keep track of the days too.

Try setting your timer for 10 minutes and lying with your eyes shut, relaxed, it seems a hell of a long time.

Anyway ... Retirement, and what it means to me?

1. No Monday morning feeling, in fact you must purposefully look at the calendar to see what day it is Ha!
2. Plenty of Annual leave and no need to ask or fit in with the other employees around you. You also get all the bank holidays off and no need to negotiate if you can have Christmas and New Year off.
3. The only policies and procedures are those set by yourself or your OCD sweetheart Lol ...
4. You don't necessarily get the same money in your pay-packet, but you don't necessarily need as much either. Remember the most important currency?
5. You don't have any issues with time to prepare meals/ housework/shopping/washing etc...
6. You can take holidays in school term times and there are very few little people spoiling the peace either ...
7. If you feel like going to the pub in the afternoon, you can ...or going on holiday when you've just come back ... you can (providing your funds allow)
8. If you want to do a course at college, you can ...
9. Learn something new or even something others would find ridiculous or eccentric ... yeah man!
10. Basically there are no rules, Why not? ... You've got one foot in the grave anyway ... who cares?

I have reached the time in my life where I only have to do work, I choose to do, where I can dedicate my time to exploring stuff I never had time to do before. It can be paid or unpaid work according to my choosing, hobbies, learning new stuff ... writing a book ... just great.

When folks ask me what I do, I tell them ... I'm a writer, artist, poet, blogger, potter, crafter, seamstress. The list is endless! Artist in residence, Writer in Chief! I MIGHT never write a million-pound best seller but who cares, I don't do it for the money, I do it for the satisfaction ... and the only person I need to satisfy is myself!

An old friend was once in a pub with one of the golden oldies (as he thought). They had a conversation about getting old

"How old are you, Jack?"
"70 next birthday"
"Eee, I hope I don't live till I'm 70"
"You will when you're 69" ... Lol
"If I'd known I was going to live this long, I'd have taken more care of myself ... "

Well it's right, you don't think about the hammer you give your knees till they don't work as well as they should ... maybe I should have thought when I sat with them bent under my legs on the settee or knelt down when I needn't have done ...

Having said all this, I wonder how I even found the time to work full time. I'm very lucky to be able to call upon my skills and still have a contribution to make. I am just in the process of writing a course of workshops to help people who want to write creatively with confidence. Not that I'm any sort of expert, but I do have the confidence to empower people to believe in themselves and for me, that's one of the major stumbling blocks in achieving your goals. Writing helps to fulfil my need to be purposeful and gives me a sense of achievement, keeps me in touch with lots of people and develops my skills at the same time. I think it's important to know that there are more positive outcomes to taking part than you may think.

Far from being the end of the road, retirement for me started on the open highway, our first trip was across Europe on our way back from Tenerife. Don't forget now your retired, you really are an adult! so don't worry what anyone thinks or says and as long as you're not hurting anyone, largely anything goes. Be confident! Hold your head high! I don't know about you, but I think I've missed a few opportunities because I overthought or doubted myself. Looking back most times you have nothing to lose by giving it a go.

In the first instance, taking the plunge returning to the UK, was a long wished for goal for me. I loved Tenerife but had outgrown it quite a few years before. It was like a weight had been lifted, a new dawn, whoop! One of my philosophies in life is that you only regret the things you didn't do, well I don't regret our Tenerife adventure, but making the decision to return to the UK was the right one.

I don't know if you have a go with the language when you visit foreign shores. Spanish people are very friendly so have confidence in yourself and learn a few Spanish Words, you'll be surprised at the response. I've had many a laugh when I've said something in Spanish and the other person has set off at pace with the reply and have burst out laughing at my face because I don't understand a word of what they say. I've found it good to learn how to say "slowly please, pardon me and sorry I don't understand" they're the most used of the phrases I know in Spanish. I happened to be on a bus only yesterday in Spain and was sat just behind the driver, the lady driver was extremely friendly, but the number of passengers who never said please or thank you even in their own language was embararasing.

Just remember the other person is Sister ... different language, like a Wiganer but from Spain?? Lol! In a few words ... Me? I'm more tomato sauce than salsa!

On 7th May 2019, we set off from Tenerife, car packed to the gunnels and headed for Santa Cruz de Tenerife and the ferry to mainland Spain. We were stopped by customs boarding the ferry looking for duty free cigs and booze. There wasn't a square inch of space in the car, the boot was topped with the frying pan which duly rolled out when the border official, determined to "search the boot" opened it up. It looked all too much of a big job for him, he sighed and waved us on. It was a great adventure up the coast of Spain, booking into places to stay as we approached. Like a pair of teenagers, we explored all the little traditional Spanish bars in the sticks for coffee.

One day, we detoured off the main road for a pit stop and landed in what could only be described as a one-horse village, not a soul on the streets. There were shutters on all the traditional Spanish terraced houses and the air was bone dry as the sun baked the street. In the distance, a woman in a headscarf and pinnie was putting chairs and tables outside what looked like a bar. As we approached, she turned and went inside and banged the door shut. It was a tall arched door, the wood looked aged and dry. Anyone who knows me wouldn't be surprised that without further ado, I took a big deep breath and lifted the latch.

"Hola Senora!" ... I called inside, as my eyes adjusted to the light, I could see several male customers sipping from small glasses of espresso coffee. Everyone in the bar raised their eyes and in anticipation, I looked over, and breathed out as the friendly Spanish lady greeted me with a smile ... Phew (I was dying for the loo, Lol) Like two natives we joined the locals for morning coffee albeit Wigan style with Milk! Our confidence grew the more stops we made ... (well mine did)

Basically, it's like your local, and a couple of Spanish people walk in, can you imagine the domino team in the Miners Arms when Manuel drops in? They would be like who the hell is this, he must be a lorry driver who's got lost Lol. No-one would have a clue how to speak Spanish, unlike most Spanish people when we visit their country, and all the Brits expect everyone to speak English ...
Moral of the story ... never be afraid to go off the beaten track, you never know what you might discover!

A little tale has just come to mind, we were on holiday in Majorca with Cousin Danny, the lovely Kathleen and the kids, on the way home from the night's revelries, fancying something to eat, we spotted McDonalds on the Prom. Making a beeline for a Big-Mac, off we went, Danny leading the charge ...
The friendly Spanish McDonald's crew member greeted Danny first ... "Hola Senor"
He gave her his order ... "Ere ya are luv give us a Big Mac"
"Perdon senor?"
"A Big Mac luv, Oh ... and clod a few chips on"
"Perdon?"
"They're bloody ignorant these Spanish, aren't they?"
Lol ... it makes me smile even now, the McDonald's crew member's face was a picture and, so I imagine was ours!

I make it a rule that wherever I go, I can at least say Hello, Goodbye, Please & Thankyou, I can do Spanish, French,

German, Polish, Russian and of course English Ha! My next one will be Norwegian for our upcoming trip. (Table 1)

One of the most memorable stops on our trip home was in Ronda, Andalusia, you would think Wales with a name like that. We drove and parked bang in the centre of the town and happened upon a B&B which were rooms above a café/restaurant. A princely £30 a night, it was hardly surprising the room had no windows, it was painted bright green and had furniture as old as the hills. A rickety wooden bed and the smell of disinfectant. Ronda is a Spanish Roman town, a feast for the senses, beautiful architecture and surrounding countryside. We were completely blown away by its beauty and atmosphere. It is certainly a place to put on the bucket list!

We stayed for only a couple of days at most on our trip to each place as we were aiming for Barcelona to see our beloved Wigan Rugby play at Nou-Camp. OMG,

Barcelona was another mind-blowing experience Gaudi's La Sagrada Familia, the biggest cathedral I've ever seen, seemed to stretch to the heavens, people below looking like the size of ants.

Successive Governments have shaved years off the time when men and women can claim the hard-earned State Pension, so folks are finding it difficult not to continue in paid employment. Personally, I'm really glad to have taken my nursing pension at 50, because I now find myself in a position where I would be unable to fulfil my role as a nurse/ Health Visitor due to my ailing health. At the time, everyone was telling me that I'd lose 40% because I was taking it early, the effect of that was in the big picture I have now collected it for 14 years already, and some of my colleagues are still working.

I'm not looking for sympathy Lol ... you could say "If you are ...you can find it between Sh*t and Syphilis in the dictionary"

I enjoy good health generally but at a slower pace. I'm lucky to have the where with all to keep myself busy and productive. After all you know what they say "If you don't use it ... You'll lose it!" I'm lucky to be able to work a few hours a week doing stuff I really enjoy, contributes to keeping me mentally in order. I had a conversation with a manager at work about availability today. Her opening Question was "Are there any months when your not taking a holiday" Lol

Personally, part of the issue for me is that your job defines your identity in Western culture, and I feel that retired people, although we may be the wisest in terms of

237

experience, culture, in my opinion, throws people on the scrap heap once retired. The government don't give us the credit we should have for what we add to the hidden economy, caring for children and our older folks being at least two of them.

It would be a great idea to set up a skills bank/ agency where older people could offer their services on a when needed basis or would fit in with the requirement of businesses who need help on an ad hoc basis. Can you imagine www.gov.uk/rentagrannie Lol! I might just set it up 😵 😊

I think the essence of staying fit and healthy in retirement is to recognise, it is not the time to sit on the sofa waiting for God. Routine is very important, so to keep yourself going. In other words, get up, make up, Dress up and show up! It makes all the difference; it keeps your life purposeful and it's a great time to do all those things you've always wanted to do. So:

- o Have a date night with your sweetheart
- o Take up a new hobby
- o Have a routine
- o Have a quiet moment in each day
- o Do a bit of work, paid or voluntary
- o Spend time with those you love
- o Visit places you have never been even if it's a short bus-ride.
- o And anything else you can fit in

On that note, I'm going to sign off, hopefully there's plenty of life in the old dog yet. I'm off to visit more places, drink more drinks, laugh at some more jokes and generally take every minute and treat it with the respect it deserves!

So far I've completed 23,256 days in the Big Mother House, here's to a few thousand more!

W

Al Si Thi ...

Well, I think I've come to the end of this little project, I've enjoyed writing it and I hope it will give anyone who cares to read it, ... a smile! If you're not mentioned, it's not because you don't mean anything to me, it's just how it's come out.

I'm not going to bore you with thankyous, loads of people influence my life in their own way, you already know who you are, and anyone who knows me will appreciate that I value you all. Have a great day, wherever you are, and remember ....

I Hope you Dance

About The Author

I'm a home bird, but I love travelling ... I'm like Busy Lizzie, always doing something or other and I love it. Once I've mastered something, I usually have to move on to something else.

That doesn't mean I can't stick to the job in hand, I worked for the same organisation for 30 years so I'm also loyal and committed. I can always find time to fit a task in if needed, you know, if you want something doing ask a busy person. Above all, I'm a human bean! I'd do a little do a little dance if you let me know what you what think about my ramblings, it makes my day!
Take a look by my blog if you have a minute at
www.millyismetresfrommadness.com
@lovingly.made.by.nan &
@onamorepositivenote
on Instagram
mariad.fedigan@gmail.com

Denise's guide to saying hello in Foreign Parts ...

Table 1

Language	Hello	Goodbye	Please	Thankyou
Spanish	Hola	Adios	Por Favor	Gracias
French	Bonjour	Au Revoir	S'il Vous Plait	Merci
German	Guten Tag	Auf Weidersehn	Bitte	Danke
Polish	Witam	Do Widzenia	Proszę	Dziękuje
Russian	Привет Pronounce privet	До свидания Pronounced Dos vidanya	Пожалуйста Pronounce pojaluista	Спасибо Pronounced spasibo

Printed in Great Britain
by Amazon

78744241R00139